CW01676510

SIGNS AND SEALS OF THE COVENANT

A REVIEW OF THE DOCTRINE OF CHRISTIAN BAPTISM

C. G. KIRKBY

"He hath made with me an everlasting Covenant" 2 Sam. 23:5.

The text of all quotations of the Holy Scriptures
is that of the Authorised Version.

Acknowledgement
Book cover designed by Sandra Littleton Evans.

First edition 1986
Revised edition 1988
Reprinted 2000

ISBN 0 9511302 1 8

Printed and bound in Great Britain by
Creative Print and Design, Wales

PREFACE

The discussion contained in the following pages relates to a subject of considerable antiquity, and one of great ambiguity, for it has been a bone of contention between God's people from the earliest days of the Christian Church. In presenting this discussion I am not unmindful of the fact that most of the arguments contained in it have been propounded before, and for this reason some people may question the need for retracing well trodden ground. There are particular circumstances, however, which prompted me to take this action.

As will be evident from the reading of these pages the interpretation of the Biblical teaching on baptism, as understood by me, is that which is normally referred to as the paedobaptist interpretation. However, being a member of an Independent Baptist Church having a Strict Baptist background, I felt under a certain moral obligation to give reasons for my interpretation of this aspect of Biblical truth, in view of its somewhat radical difference from that held by Strict Baptists. Consequently I undertook to prepare a written statement, not contemplating at the outset a particularly lengthy document. However, having embarked on the task, it became evident to me that as this matter had been the subject of debate over the long years of the history of the Christian Church, it could not be adequately presented without being seen against its historical background and in its relation to the Church.

It will be observed therefore that some space has been given to this historical aspect, both regarding God's dealings with mankind from the dawn of history onwards, and also regarding the attitudes and beliefs of men with respect to the subject of

Christian baptism. In this connection also, some space has been given to a consideration of the nature of the Church, the "Covenant of Grace" and the signs and seals of the Covenant.

In presenting an interpretation of this subject, an attempt has been made to avoid the influences of traditional viewpoints, and to re-examine the ground on which our views are based. Inevitably, and it is felt correctly, in order to do this, not only have the essential meanings of the words of Scripture been considered, but also the exposition of the text and the context.

Some of the main sources of information consulted in preparing this treatise are given below and grateful acknowledgement is made of the great help which they have yielded.

Christian Baptism	— John Murray
Romans — Exposition of Ch. 6 — The New Man	— D. M. Lloyd-Jones
Colossians — Exposition of Ch. 2	— Wm. Hendrikson
Works — Volumes 3 & 6	— John Flavel (Puritan)
The Church Membership of Children	— Thomas Shepard (Puritan)
Heaven Opened	— Richard Alleine (Puritan)
Collected Writings Vol 3	— J. H. Thornwell (19th century)
Knots Untied	— J. C. Ryle (19th century)
Historical Theology	— Wm. Cunningham (19th century)
A History of Christianity	—Kenneth Scott Latourette
The New International Dictionary of the Christian Church	— Published by Paternoster Press
The Oxford Dictionary of the Christian Church	— Published by The Oxford University Press

Studies in Theology Vol. 9 — B. B. Warfield

Works — Vol. 1 — John Bunyan (Puritan)

My plea to readers of these pages is that they would deliberately put to one side any prejudices and preconceived notions with regard to the subject of this treatise, and give careful and prayerful consideration to the Scriptural evidence herein presented. This plea not being with intent that one side should be seen to be right and the other seen to be wrong, but rather with the heartfelt desire that we *all* might come to the truth in this matter, as in every other point of Christian doctrine, so as to eliminate a major barrier to universal Christian communion and unity. My prayer to God for us all is that He would be pleased to shed more and more light upon His glorious Word, in the power of His Spirit, in all its aspects, "till we all come in the unity of the faith, and of the knowledge of the Son of God, unto a perfect man (the Church of Christ), unto the measure of the stature of the fulness of Christ" (Eph.4: 13).

PREFACE TO THE SECOND EDITION

It has been very gratifying to me to receive, from some readers, observations relating to statements contained in this book. And as it is quite possible that others may share the views expressed in those observations, it seemed that they might profitably be included in this second edition, together with a response to the points raised, in the form of an Appendix.

The only other change made in this revised edition is to the General Index, which has been entirely recast.

''All too often in recent years it has been customary for us to act as though the Gospel could prosper on earth independently of the conditions of the visible Church; and evangelicals have been content to meet in organisations and societies as though the denominational differences which divide them are incapable of any scriptural solution. — A common attachment to the Scriptures and a determination to seek grace to resolve difficulties in that light is the only sure basis of Church unity.''

From ''The Reformation of the Church'' (1965). Iain H. Murray.

CONTENTS

INTRODUCTION

We are living in days of confusion and perplexity in the realm of the Christian Church, and this situation seems to have arisen as a result of the effects of different factors influencing the minds of God's people. Some are aware of a spirit of apathy which has apparently settled down over large areas of the universal Church, resulting in its unattractive deadness and irrelevance in the eyes of the world. As a reaction to this situation some have sought to devise means of injecting relevance and attractiveness into the Church's image, hoping that thereby the world would be drawn into the Church and in this way be influenced for good. "Why are so few, from the world, joining the Church?" was asked by someone at the beginning of this century. "Because so many in the Church are joining the world"*, was the answer given! So we see that this is no new trouble that the Church is experiencing today.

There is an awareness amongst God's people that we are failing to influence the world in the way in which God intends us to do. We see the world "on fire", spiritually speaking, and yet the Church seems to be in a condition of impotence in respect of any restraining influence it might have upon the nations of the world. We see this; and yet when we look at ourselves we realise that we are not all pulling in the same direction, and this results in the neutralisation of the various efforts and endeavours put forth. The great Prophet of God's people has set down in Holy Writ a principle which need not be excluded from the realm of the Christian Church. "Every kingdom divided against itself is brought to desolation" (Luke 11:17); if we divide one from

*"The Twofold Life" by A. J. Gordon.

another, we become an easy prey to our common enemy. Our great adversary Satan is well able to employ the fraility of men in producing confusion and ineffectiveness in the ranks of God's people.

Satan uses many devices to *divide* and neutralise the energies of the saints. God uses only one means to *unite* them and that is His Word. It is only too evident to-day that man, almost intuitively, recognises the advantages to be derived from unity. We see this principle operating in industry, both in the realm of management and of labour. The one is revealed in mergers and confederations, the other in trade unions. We see it in national and international politics. But nowhere have moves towards union been more relentlessly and pathetically pursued than in the realm of religion. Religious leaders have met in their conferences to seek a formula which would form the basis of agreement and unity; and this has necessitated the deliberate employment of ambiguous statements capable of carrying more than one meaning on which the maximum number of people may agree.

As we know, the only formula for unity is that which God has given to us in His Word. However, although we recognise the great desirability of unity amongst God's people, we must not even make *that* unity our prime objective, but rather see it as the inevitable result of a reverence for God's Word, a diligent study of it and an earnest desire to understand it more perfectly. In the same way every organisation and section of the Christian Church must be subordinate to the teaching of the Scriptures and a concentration upon a study of them. Recognising always, that a study of the Scriptures could be merely an activity of the mind; but the study that leads to unity is that which results from a saving faith in the Lord Jesus Christ, which has a tendency, by the very nature of the new life created thereby, to produce a unifying desire for the sincere milk of the Word. This must be the Church's priority, and then all other things, particularly the usefulness of the Church in the world, will flow out of it as out of a "well of living waters".

In the light of the unquestioned desirability of this true unity amongst God's people, it becomes a matter of great importance that we take note of those things which stand in the way of the universal and complete unity of the Christian Church today, and having identified them we must then decide whether they should be allowed to continue to exercise a divisive influence in the Church as they do at the present time.

It is not my intention to enumerate these things, it would only be invidious to do so, but they must be self-evident. However, with this general objective in mind, the purpose of this present treatise is to look at one particular subject, which by its very nature has proved to be at the foundation of many differences which have arisen in the Church over the past centuries, namely the subject of Christian baptism.

The method which I have adopted in reviewing this subject is as follows. We will first consider its historical background. It seems to me that as the whole of the Christian revelation is steeped in history, it is essential, if we are to understand any aspect of Christian truth fully, to look at it in its historical setting. It is a living truth, revealed by a living God for living men. Not only are we interested in its origins, which interest is paramount, but also in its impact upon succeeding generations of mankind. We will then consider the doctrinal basis of our subject, looking at what the Scriptures tell us with regard to its purpose in God's great plan of redemption. This will inevitably necessitate a consideration of certain allied subjects such as the nature of the Church, God's covenants with His people and the signs and seals of the Covenant of Grace. We will give particular attention to the crucial matter of infant baptism, considering also the mode of baptism. We will finally examine the Reformed Baptist understanding of this subject, and its application to the local church situation.

Whereas this treatise represents a theological review, nevertheless, on account of its intensely personal and practical implications, the reader will detect, throughout, certain inevitable pastoral undertones.

★ ★ ★

''That department of the history of the Church which affords the most ample materials for assisting in the understanding of the system of Christian theology, is just the history of the Church since the completed revelation of God's will was put into its hands, and especially the history of the principal discussions which have taken place in regard to its meaning and import. The history of the way in which the Church has used this revelation, and of the discussions which have taken place concerning its meaning, are fitted, when rightly used and applied, to afford us important assistance in forming a correct estimate of what it is really adapted and intended to communicate and to effect.''

From ''Historical Theology'' (1862) by William Cunningham.

HISTORICAL BACKGROUND

If we would understand, and fully appreciate the meaning and significance of any particular point of truth, as we have it revealed in the Scriptures, we must consider it in its historical setting. We must see first of all its source and origin, in order to discover the reason for its existence. If we would understand the doctrine of regeneration, we must go back to the dawn of history and find out why it was that such a provision was ever made by God, whereupon we discover that at the beginning of time, after God had completed His work of Creation, and after He had surveyed the works of His hands and declared them to be very good, it was *then,* upon that idyllic stage, that ''sin entered, and death by sin'' (Rom.5:12). So man became spiritually dead, and if he were to escape eternal death then there was a clear necessity for him to be brought to life again. Here we find the situation which has necessitated, and by God's grace introduced, the work of regeneration.

So it is with every Scriptural truth, every point of doctrine, concerning which we would have as full an understanding as possible, we must trace it back to its source, not stopping even at the beginning of the Christian era, but going back, if needs be, to the beginning of time.

In the case of the subject before us, in order to appreciate the significance of Christian baptism, we must go back to the beginning to discover the reason why God introduced it, and what purpose He intended it to serve in relation to His unchanging plan of redemption. In this connection we must recognise the fact that God's plan for the redemption of guilty sinners is operative throughout the whole of time, and applicable to all sinners of all eras. The plan, in its essence, has never changed throughout the various dispensations of God's dealings with mankind. In other words, the Old Testament saint is not to be regarded as a "second class saint" on account of the fact that in his day the Redeemer had not yet been crucified on the cross of Calvary. We can be sure that every one of the Old Testament saints is "accepted in the Beloved", and only in Him. Abraham (for instance) rejoiced to see the day of Christ's work of salvation when He was here in the flesh. Abraham saw it by faith and this sight gladdened his heart. He knew that the salvation of his immortal soul depended upon the work of God's promised Messiah. God said to Abraham "in thy seed shall *all the nations of the earth* be blessed" (Gen.26:4) which promise Paul shows refers to Christ — "And to thy *seed,* which is Christ" (Gal.3:16).

So we come to recognise the fact that throughout the whole of the period covered by the Old Testament a number of individuals trusted in the saving work of the *coming* Messiah for their soul's eternal salvation. They were saved people—saints—every bit as much as those living in the New Testament period, and up to the present time, who have put their trust in the *crucified* Messiah. These Old Testament saints are members of the Church of the living God.

We shall have occasion later to consider in rather more detail the nature of the Church, because of its importance in relation to the subject before us, but it is sufficient, for our present purpose, for us to be aware of this principle of continuity and invariableness in God's gracious dealings with sinners throughout the ages.

The Bible opens, as we know, with that arresting phrase "In the beginning God....". God acted, and brought into being a whole universe, including this world, and created man and made him to have dominion over the works of His hands and put all things under his feet. This was God's first revelation of His great plan for the part that man should play in His universe. God freely and voluntarily entered into a covenant with Adam, His newly created man, which has been referred to as the "Covenant of Works". There was a condition attached to this Covenant, requiring the obedience of Adam to God's commandments. Then man rebelled against God, and so the Covenant was broken, and man's previously enjoyed and promised benefits were forfeited.

If God were to enter into a new covenant, to replace the old, it could not be with Adam, for he had been manifestly discredited. Consequently a second Adam was revealed to mankind, and God entered into a new Covenant with Him, namely His own Son, which has been referred to as the "Covenant of Grace". This Covenant, thenceforward, became the basis of all God's merciful dealings with the fallen, sinful, guilty human race.

I will defer any doctrinal consideration of this Covenant of Grace until later. It will suffice for our present purpose to notice the principle involved, in that by means of this Covenant God gave assurance to the fallen race of mankind that in spite of the culpability of man as the result of the fall, He showed Himself to be "merciful and gracious, long-suffering, and abundant in goodness and truth". "Wherein He hath abounded toward us in all wisdom and prudence; having made known unto us the mystery of His will, according to His good pleasure which He hath purposed in Himself" (Ex.34:6; Eph.1:8,9). Whereas the generally accepted understanding of a covenant is that it is a pact between two parties who are on an equal footing, nevertheless in the case of a covenant between God and man this condition quite obviously does not pertain. In the same way the first Covenant, the Covenant of Works, included the requirement on the part of man, of obedience; the second Covenant, the Covenant of Grace, also included a requirement on the part of man, a requirement to exercise faith. The central promise on God's part in this Covenant of Grace is "I will be a God unto thee". God gives reminders of this through His unfolding revelation in such places as Gen. 17:7,8; Ex.6:7; Ex.29:45; Lev.26:12; Jer.24:7; Jer.31:33; 2 Cor.6:18; Heb.8:10; Rev.21:3,7.

From this we see that God has an unchanging, consistent, purpose of grace towards guilty sinners, which has been operating from the earliest days, ever since God declared His purpose after man rebelled against Him, having been tempted by Satan, when He made the first shadowy reference to His plan for redeeming fallen man by the sacrifice of the Son of man on the Cross; whom, He had appointed "to be a Prince and a Saviour" (Acts 5:31); as we find it foretold in Gen.3:15—The Saviour would bruise Satan's head 'that through death He might destroy him that had the power of death, that is, the devil'' (Heb.2:14). This unchanging plan of God, as contained in His Covenant of Grace, has been operating from the earliest days of history right down to this present time, and will continue to operate until the end of time and beyond into the countless ages of eternity.

★ ★ ★

"There is perhaps no subject in Christianity about which such difference of opinion exists as the sacrament of baptism. The very name recalls to one's mind an endless list of strifes, disputes, heart-burnings, controversies, and divisions. It is a subject, moreover, on which even eminent Christians have long been greatly divided. Praying, Bible-reading, holy men, who can agree on all other points, find themselves hopelessly divided about baptism."

From "Knots Untied" (1877) by J. C. Ryle.

THE HISTORY OF BAPTISM

Whereas the supremacy and sufficiency of the sacred Scriptures, as the only real standard for faith and practice, must always be maintained, there is, nevertheless, undoubted benefit to be derived from a careful study of the history of the Church subsequent to the period covered by the canon of Holy Scripture. The subsequent history of the Church provides us with the principal discussions which have taken place regarding the meaning and import of the system of Christian theology revealed in the Scriptures. In this history we see how godly, but fallible, men have grappled with the various doctrines of the Christian faith; sometimes with unhappy results. It is also instructive as it reveals to us how, from time to time, God has raised up outstanding men, to whom He imparted unusual gifts, who have contended for the faith, and brought the straying Church back onto its proper course. This is not the occasion to enlarge on the subject but it should be noted in passing that examples of these outstanding Church leaders can be found in such men as Athanasius (C.300–373), Augustine (c.354–430), Luther (c.1483–1546) and Calvin (c.1509–1564).

Our present purpose, however, is to discover the attitudes and practices, that have been adopted by the Church down through the running centuries. As we do so, we can bear in mind that the Church has always comprised people such as ourselves, earnestly seeking to interpret the teaching of Holy Writ, and to put such interpretations into practice, in the life of the Church, and where necessary embodying such interpretations in confessions, in records of Church Counsels and in Catechisms. Not that they considered such documents to supersede in authority the inspired declarations of Scripture, but, in the light of previous contentions within the Church, believing it to be advantageous to systematise and summarise some of the basic truths which they had discovered in God's Word.

It appears from the history of the Church that the fathers, so called, began at a very early stage to talk about the subject of the sacraments in an exalted, mysterious and unintelligible style, which was very far removed from the simplicity of the Scriptures. These early views had a very destructive influence on the life of true religion in the Church. In this connection we see the danger of putting too much emphasis on the antiquity of the traditions of the early Church, which is one of the dangerous practices of the Roman Catholic Church.

Protestants in general have freely conceded that the doctrine and practice of the Church in regard to the sacraments was at an early period, covering say the first three centuries, considerably corrupted, particularly as relating to erroneous and exaggerated notions of the virtue and efficacy of the sacramental elements. This had a far-reaching and detrimental effect on the purity of the doctrine and practice of the Church. These erroneous views of the sacraments rebounded on the Church's avowal of the fundamental doctrines of the Gospel, as the sign was largely substituted, by outward observances, for the thing signified. Thus was introduced a belief in some inherent power or efficacy of the ordinances themselves, irrespective of the faith and character of the recipient.

Before the end of the third century the fathers referred to baptism as being equated with the remission of sin, and at the same time with the renovation of the moral nature. At first, this was on the assumption of the exercise of existing faith, but the emphasis was placed more and more on the baptism and less and less on the faith. And so at length baptism virtually abolished the great fundamental principle of justification by faith, which was kept in the background until it was brought to light again by Martin Luther. Certainly the leading writers were, before the end of the fourth century, maintaining the absolute necessity of baptism to salvation, both in infants and adults, which error led to a belief in what has since been called "baptismal regeneration".

Even Justin, commonly called Justin Martyr, in the second century, taught baptismal regeneration, basing his view on John 3:5 and Isaiah 1:16–20. The Church of Rome still teaches both that baptism cleanses from all past sins, and that it is indispensably necessary to salvation.

Infant baptism was practised in the second century but only with the aid of a sponsor. Augustine defended this in the late 4th and early 5th centuries. In the 5th century the Syrian Church made infant baptism obligatory; prior to this it seems to have been the exception rather than the rule in that Church. From the 5th century onwards the importance of infant baptism placed great stress upon the rite being administered prior to the eighth day after birth.

By the end of the 5th century the practice in Rome was for the newly baptised infants to be brought to a special chapel behind the baptistry and there the Pope prayed to God to send His Holy Spirit on them, and, dipping his thumb in some consecrated oil, he made the sign of the cross on the forehead of each saying "In the name of the Father, and the Son, and the Holy Spirit peace to you".

By the 10th century baptism of the infant offspring of Christian parents had become universal and it was believed to effect the new birth and was therefore thought to be necessary for salvation. Infants dying unbaptised, so it was held, being still tainted with original sin, would not go to heaven. Children were accordingly to be baptised as soon as possible after birth. The ceremony might be by immersion or by affusion, namely by water being poured over the child as the sponsor held it over the font.

Martin Luther recognised the value of baptism and did not deny it to infants. He held that it is done, not by man, but by the Trinity through a man. But he also wrote that unless a man has faith, it profits him nothing. Baptism in itself, he declared, does not justify, but only faith in the Word of promise, to which baptism is added. Although when baptised, the infants are not able to exercise faith, Luther said that they are aided by the faith of those who bring them to baptism. It was in connection with this aspect of baptism that Luther, and those referred to as Anabaptists, parted company. The Swiss theologian Zwingli (1484–1531), like Luther, taught that salvation is by faith alone, and they both saw baptism to be a sign only, and unnecessary to salvation.

John Calvin has left a very clear record in his "Institutes of the Christian Religion", of all the leading doctrines of the Christian faith, including his understanding of the ordinance of baptism. He writes:

"Baptism contributes to our faith three things. The first object for which it is appointed by the Lord, is to be a sign and evidence of our purification. In this sense is to be understood the statement of Paul that 'Christ loved the Church, and gave Himself for it, that He might sanctify and cleanse it with the washing of water by the Word' (Eph.5: 25,26). Another benefit of baptism is, that it shows us our mortification in Christ and new life in Him. The third advantage which our faith receives from baptism is its assuring us not only that we are engrafted into the death and life of Christ, but so united to Christ Himself as to be partakers of all His blessings." (Book 4. Chapter 15).

In about 1524, in Germany, many of the churches declared their independence as congregations of believers, and their determination to observe and to carry out, as churches, the teaching of Scripture. Congregations had done the same sort of thing in 1467 at a place called Lhota in central Europe. In both places, as they were assembled together, they baptised all those present by immersion. In the case of those in Germany this gave rise to a new name, the Anabaptists, meaning "Re-baptisers". Their refusal to admit that infant baptism was true baptism led to them being given this nickname. It is the comprehensive designation of various groups on the Continent who in the 16th century refused to allow their children to be baptised, and who re-instituted the baptism of believers; whereas the majority of Christians at that time regarded the baptism of infants as a most important Christian ordinance and as a means of initiation into the Church.

These groups of Anabaptists, variously called the radicals or left wing of the Reformation, emerged on the religious scene independently and without collusion, and displayed a marked variety. This variety of expression has resulted in their identity, as recorded in the annals of the Church, becoming blurred and indefinite. This fact may perhaps be better understood by glancing briefly at some of the more significant groups.

One group was associated with Thomas Müntzer, who was regarded as one of its more violent representatives. He sought to gather the elect into churches and to set them to slaughtering the ungodly and those who honoured images. Luther was appalled at this and urged the princes of Saxony to prevent such a use of the sword. Müntzer was thought to be the major fomenter of a revolt in Saxony around 1524–1525.

From 1525 to 1528 the movement became very strong in Germany, especially in Strasburg and Augsburg. Its members were often accused of being revolutionary and plotting treasonable activities against the State, and were unjustly maligned in many ways. The Diet of Speier in 1529 approved an imperial mandate of the previous year that re-baptisers, and the re-baptised, should be put to death, even without proper forms of trial. It is reckoned that within a few years no less than 2000 people perished due to this mandate. At first, Luther strongly opposed such persecuting methods, but as the Anabaptist movement spread he became alarmed and, in 1530, urged "the use of the sword against them by right of law".

Another group of Anabaptists existed in Zurich, known as the Swiss Brethren, which was associated with Conrad Grebel (c.1498–1526). Grebel, together with Felix Manz, led a radical movement in the city of Zurich. In Zurich Grebel came into contact with Zwingli; and was converted around 1522–1523. It was around Grebel that there gathered what were known as the Swiss Brethren. It was in connection with the subject of baptism that they came into conflict with the Zurich authorities, and in January 1525 the city council decided to stand by infant baptism and ordered Grebel and the Brethren to discontinue their movement. Grebel, Manz and others were later arrested, tried by the civil authorities in Zurich, and condemned to life imprisonment. After some months they escaped, but later, Manz was recaptured and was executed on 25th January 1527; apparently the first martyr to the Anabaptist cause. It appears that the council of the city of Zurich passed cruel and unjust laws against the Anabaptists, and most of their leaders at that time suffered the penalty of death.

Another group of Anabaptists were known as the Hutterites, or Hutterian Brethren, taking their name from Jacob Hutter, who was tortured and burned to death in 1536. For several generations these Anabaptists practised the principle of community of goods. They were especially strong in Moravia and suffered severely in the Thirty Years' War (1618 – 1648). Remnants took refuge in Hungary, and late in the eighteenth century many of them settled in south Russia.

The largest body of Anabaptists which survived the persecutions on the Continent was that known by the name of Mennonites. They took their name from Menno Simons (1496 – 1561). In 1524 Simons was consecrated priest in the Roman Catholic Church, but within a year of his ordination he had doubts about the efficacy of the Mass. He had begun a careful study of the Bible when the execution of an Anabaptist in his native West Friesland deeply shocked him, and he came to the conclusion that his own Church, and Luther, Zwingli and Calvin were wrong in practising infant baptism and that only believers' baptism had Scriptural authority. Yet he disapproved of the Anabaptists of Munster and believed that they, and the followers of Hoffmann were in error in appealing to the sword in self defence. However their heroism under persecution smote his conscience for his acceptance of ease and security in his priestly post. On 30th January 1536 he publicly renounced his Roman Catholic connection and not long afterwards was baptised. He was ordained as an Anabaptist minister and for years lived in the Netherlands as a fugitive and an outlaw under condemnation of death. Tens of thousands of Dutch Anabaptists died during this period in a wave of persecution resulting from the action of extremists. From this persecution emerged the Mennonites. By the time of his death Menno Simons had become the outstanding leader of the Anabaptists in the Netherlands and North Germany.

As can be appreciated from the foregoing, historians have found it difficult to give a comprehensive description of the Anabaptists which would cover all. Generally speaking, they expected the speedy return of Christ, rejected completely the idea of a State Church, and possessed boundless enthusiasm which sometimes carried them to extremes. The late Professor W.P. Paterson of Edinburgh admirably summed up the position in this way: "It has been made clear that the Protestant tradition judged this movement by its worst examples, ignored the ethical idealism which entered into their dreams, and passed an "anathema" on *all,* which was only merited by a few. It is, indeed, one of the tragedies of history that men like Hubmaier and Denck, and a great company of victims who followed them to the slaughter, should have been involved in the same condemnation with Müntzer and John of Leyden''.

These Anabaptists became prophetic of free church life in our own time, and ancestors of the present day Baptists. The Separatists, or Independents, in our own Country, like the Anabaptists on the Continent, believed in ''gathered'' churches; not made up of all the inhabitants of a particular area, but only of those who were conscientiously Christian. They believed that they should be united with one another and with Christ in a covenant. Each congregation so united, with Christ as its Head, was a self-governing church, which elected its own pastor and other officers, after what was believed to be the pattern discernible in the New Testament. They were Separatists in that they withdrew from the Church of England, and were Independents in that they believed in the full autonomy of each local church. Although they were still small minorities they continued to grow. Persecuted, some sought refuge on the Continent, especially in Protestant Holland, but many remained in England.

In 1609 John Smyth's English Separatist congregation, in exile in Amsterdam, was led by a study of the New Testament, to disband and reorganise itself, with believers' baptism as the basis of church fellowship. It held Arminian views, and was the spiritual ancestor of the General Baptists of Britain. Smyth, and most of his congregation, applied to join the Mennonites, and were accepted by them in 1615. Meanwhile, Thomas Helwys, and a small group under him, who broke with Smyth, returned to England in 1612 and founded what seems to have been the first Baptist Church on English soil, at Spitalfields, and took pains to disassociate himself from the Mennonites. A few years later what were known as Particular Baptists arose, so designated because they held to a restricted, or particular, atonement, which was only for the elect. The two strains of Baptist Churches, General and Particular, Arminian and Calvinist, continued apart until late in the 19th century. The first Particular (or Calvinist) Baptist Church came into being between 1633 and 1638 as a secession from the Independent Jacob–Lathrop–Jessey Church: so named from its succession of pastors.

The Baptists maintained that children should not be baptised, but at first the mode of baptism for adults was by affusion or sprinkling, but by about 1633 immersion became general. From the earliest times there were Baptists who believed in "mixed" or open communion. John Bunyan, whose views on this subject we will be considering more fully in a later section, was the pastor of a church consisting of Baptists and paedobaptists.

The writings of Andrew Fuller, particularly his "The Gospel Worthy of All Acceptation" (1785) helped to break down the extreme Calvinism then common among them. It was among Particular Baptists of moderate Calvinistic convictions, that in 1792, spurred on by William Carey (who in turn had been influenced by Andrew Fuller), the ministers of the Northamptonshire Association formed the Baptist Missionary Society.

A "General Union" of Particular Baptist ministers and churches was formed in 1813, and has been known since 1873 as the Baptist Union of Great Britain and Ireland.

Orthodox and evangelical Baptists had formed a New Connexion in 1770, but in 1891 this New Connexion and the Baptist Union merged.

The Baptists constitute one of the largest free church communions, with a world membership in 1971 of over 31 million, which is equivalent to a little more than 1% of the world's total population.

★ ★ ★

"Walk about Zion, and go round about her: tell the towers thereof. Mark ye well her bulwarks, (ponder and consider whether these spiritual bulwarks are likely to hold out, or not, against the certain attack by the Church's enemies) consider her palaces; that ye may tell it to the generation following. For this God is our God (in covenant) for ever and ever."

Psalm 48:12–14.

"I will build My Church; and the gates of hell shall not prevail against it."

Matt.16:18.

Christ's love for, and opinion of, His bride the Church — "Thou art beautiful, O My love, as Tirzah, comely as Jerusalem, terrible as an army with banners. Turn away thine eyes from Me, for they have overcome Me", or, "they are taking Me by storm".

Song of Solomon 6:4, 5.

"And I John saw the holy city, new Jerusalem, coming down from God out of heaven, prepared as a bride adorned for her husband."

Rev.21:2.

THE CHURCH

I have already made reference to the aspect of the unity, continuity and universality of the nature of the Church, from the dawn of history, down to the present time. This you will remember is deduced from the fact that all the members of the Church attribute their membership to their faith in the substitutionary sacrifice of the Lord Jesus Christ upon the Cross of Calvary. Man, as the result of his rebellion against God, in the garden of Eden, in disobeying His express commands, placed himself under the wrath and the judgment of God. As a consequence of this act of rebellion a universal blight came upon the whole human race, without a single exception. As far as man was concerned this situation was an "impasse"; he was utterly "without hope"; and if the situation had been allowed by God to rest there, the whole human race would have been assigned to everlasting destruction, as the inevitable and automatic and causal succession of his rebellion.

Nevertheless, God intervened; and according to His sovereign good pleasure, He published, for the first time, His promise of deliverance, which promise is the foundation of the Church. God published it Himself, immediately, as we have it described in Gen.3:15, which was the first shadowy reference to His plan for redeeming a people for Himself, and was the first publication of His Covenant of Grace.

The Covenant of Grace and the Church are inextricably bound up together. The former, which will be dealt with more fully later, is an agreement, so to speak, between God and all believers in Christ. It describes certain benefits which God, of His own good pleasure, purposes to bestow upon a specific people. Those people comprise the Church, and so we see how it is that the Covenant of Grace is bonded to the Church.

This first faint outline of His Covenant of Grace was explained, confirmed, expanded and declared throughout the subsequent pages of Holy Writ and confirmed again by the Lord Jesus Christ. Although it must be admitted that the revelation of God's grace was more obscure in the days of the early patriarchs, before the flood, nevertheless there is little doubt that they were even then, particularly and safely guided by a prophetical spirit, concerning which we have a hint in reference to Enoch in Jude 14:15. God's Covenant of Grace, restated in many promises through succeeding generations, was confirmed by the Lord Jesus Christ Himself, as Paul tells us in Rom.15:8. He "was a minister of the circumcision" — He had come to minister to the Jews, to confirm and accomplish "the promises made unto the fathers". But happily we see from verse 9 that His ministry was not limited to the Jews, for we read that He came also "that the Gentiles might glorify God for His mercy." Notice from the divine record how God made a gradual discovery of Christ from the time of Adam down through the running centuries to the New Testament times. It was revealed to Adam that He should be the Seed of the woman — but it was not revealed of what nation until Abraham's time; nor of what tribe until Jacob's time; nor of what family until David's time; nor that He should be born of a virgin until Isaiah's time; nor in what town until Micah's time.

All the promises and comforts of the Gospel are gathered into the Covenant of Grace which God subsequently confirmed to Abraham by an oath, in order to give a strong consolation and assurance of the certainty that God would keep His Covenant.

Our purpose in this section is not to consider the *nature* of the Covenant of Grace, but only to have the fact clear in our minds that God did, of His own free will, *establish* such a Covenant; like a sort of storehouse of all His promises, by which He covenanted to perform certain things for his people, and at the same time required a condition from them upon which depended their receipt of such blessings. This condition was the exercise of faith. Suffice it for our present purpose to observe that, as there was only one Covenant of Grace, so there was only one party on man's side to whom this Covenant has ever applied, and that party is the Church of God. ''As there is but one God and Father of all, one Lord over all, and one Spirit: so there is but one truth, one faith, one salvation, one Church, called in one hope, joined in one profession, guided by one rule, even the word of the Most High'' (Henry Barrow, 1589).

Because of the far-reaching importance of understanding the true nature of the Church we will now proceed to consider this subject more directly, and in a little more detail, for we find that the establishment of the Church is implicit in all of God's gracious dealings with the fallen race of mankind.

Perhaps we might clarify our *objectives* here by briefly glancing at the situation with which we are familiar to-day. Within the grouping of Christian churches we are faced with a multiplicity of denominations, each having their own characteristics, differentiated by particular opinions concerning Church government and such matters as the sacraments. The question that inevitably arises in this context is this. Do each of these denominations consider that they represent the true Church? And as a corollary, is it to be presumed that the other denominations do *not* represent the true Church? But if this is *not* the case, then the next question that must be asked is this. If the characteristics of the various different denominations do not claim to distinguish them as being, exclusively, the true Church, then what purpose do the different denominational characteristics serve? and do they not rather tend to blur the *conception* of the true Church? No doubt such a line of consideration can only lead inevitably to the admission that the absence of uniformity in the administration of the Church, as it is related to the elementary principles discovered in the churches of the New Testament, is due to our general failure, over the centuries, to understand fully the Biblical teaching with regard to this central and all important matter.

Those who have taken the teaching of God's Holy Scriptures seriously, and have recognised them to be supernatural revelation, constituting the sole authority for determining the worship and conduct of the Church, have, over the centuries, enquired and searched diligently into these Scriptures, in order to discover God's will for the detailed ordering of the life of the Church, relating to its government and outward ceremonies. After their searching, with earnest prayers to Almighty God, they have reached differing conclusions, and it forms no part of the purpose of this treatise to introduce arguments in support of any such conclusions.

Due to this situation, and an inevitable disagreement on this point amongst God's people, and as a natural consequence, they adopted the only alternative course open to them. As some form of organisation, and system of worship, and statement of faith, was necessary, in order that local churches could function properly, and that all things might be done "decently and in order", on account of the fact that universal agreement could not be reached, those who *were* in agreement joined together, subjecting themselves to the disciplines which they considered to be warranted by Scripture, and in this way polarised into various separate denominations, *each* being persuaded that their organisation was the one that enjoyed full Scriptural warrant. Based on this analysis we can but conclude that the present subdivisions of the Church into denominations can only be viewed as "second best" and something inferior to a situation in which the Church displays a uniform face to the world. And that *this* objective is that which is implicit in the Scriptures as the purpose of God, will, I think, receive universal accord.

The foregoing analysis might appear to be a somewhat negative approach, in the absence of any positive alternative; and this treatise is not intended, in any way, to present any such alternative. However, such a glance at the present visible face of the Church might perhaps urge us to "read our title deeds" again and seek with all diligence by God's grace and by the teaching and prompting of His Spirit, to understand what God has told us about His Church in His utterly reliable and inerrant Word.

I have already stated that the Church has existed from the very dawn of history,—and even from before time, as indicated in 2 Tim.1:9—"which was given us in Christ Jesus before the world began" (or "before times of ages"). This "grace" was given to us—or designated for us. The word "us" can only mean the Church, which thus has a super creation subsistence, and the individual members of the Church have common and uniform characteristics, whether they lived in the days of the Old Testament or those of the New. The common ground upon which all have stood, is, an awareness of the guilt of sin due to the fall of man, an acknowledgment of a full satisfaction having been made by God, in the Person of the promised Messiah, for the debt incurred by man for the punishment due on account of that sin, and a personal thankful *acceptance* of the satisfaction that God has provided.

Digging even deeper into God's Word, in order to uncover the foundation of the Church, we discover that "the Church's one foundation is Jesus Christ our Lord". "Other foundation can no man lay than that is laid, which is Jesus Christ" (1 Cor.3:11). "Thus saith the Lord GOD, Behold, I lay in Zion for a foundation a stone, a tried stone, a precious corner stone, a sure foundation" (Is.28:16).

But the most sublime conception that God has given to us in His Word with regard to the identity of the Church is that it is the mystical body of Christ "He is the Head of the body, the Church" (Col.1:18). The ultimate factor which determines whether or not a person is a member of the true Church is whether or not that person is united to the Lord Jesus Christ, and only the Holy Spirit can effect this union. "As in Adam all die, even so in Christ shall all be made alive" (1 Cor.15:22). Union with Adam is the cause of death; union with Christ is the cause of life. As Adam is the federal head and representative of the whole race of natural mankind, without exception, so, likewise, Christ is the federal head and representative of every one of His blood-bought people to whom has been given a new nature.

None should dispute that when Paul said "in Adam all die" he meant every person that has ever been born into this world, from Adam to the present time, and that when he said "in Christ shall all be made alive" he meant all those individuals whom the Father had given to Christ in order that He might give them eternal life (John 17:2) and *only* them. And these individuals include people who lived in the Old Testament period as well as people who live in the New Testament period. As there is only one Christ, the foundation, so there is only one Church, the superstructure.

The notion inherent in the concept of the Church is that it comprises a specific number of people, which, according to God's own good pleasure, He purposed in Himself, chose before the foundation of the world, and during the process of the unfolding of the mystery of His will, He has called out from this present evil world, purchasing them for Himself with His own blood.

The Greek term used in the New Testament for the Church is EKKLESIA, meaning literally "that which is called out". "Church" denoting the society of human beings "called out" from the fallen world into vital union with the glorified Christ as the Head of the body. Now the Hebrew term which is used in the Old Testament, and which corresponds to this Greek term, is QAHAL, which stands for an assembly of those who were called or invited. This Hebrew term is variously translated "assembly", "company", "congregation' and "multitude". In the Greek Septuagint [see also Page 100] version of the Old Testament the Greek term EKKLESIA was frequently used to represent the Hebrew term QAHAL. The first instance of this use is in Deut. 4:10 where Moses at the end of his life and on the verge of Jordan, is rehearsing all that God had done for the children of Israel, and here in particular is reminding them what God had said to him at Mount Sinai — "Gather me the people together, and I will make them hear My words, that they may learn to fear Me all the days that they shall live upon the earth, and that they may teach their children". A most important Scripture, being another publication of God's Covenant of Grace, embracing, as we see, God's people and their children.

Other passages of Scripture could be referred to, but perhaps what has been said already will be sufficient to open this window into the purposes of God as recorded in the Old Testament. The "assembly" is the Covenant people of God gathered before Him. The Covenant of God [see also Page 43] and the Church of God are inseparable, and this must be appreciated in order to obtain a clear and balanced view of God's great scheme of redemption. "Now therefore, if ye will obey My voice indeed, and keep My Covenant, then ye shall be a peculiar treasure unto Me above all people" (Ex.19: 5). This Scripture is very recognisably reflected in the words of the apostle Peter — "Ye are a chosen generation, a royal priesthood, an holy nation, a peculiar people" (1 Peter 2: 9). — showing how God's attitude towards His people in the Old Testament era was the same as His attitude towards His people in the New.

Perhaps two more passages of Scripture will help to establish the unity and universality of "the Church of the living God"

(1 Tim 3:15) — A people, said God, which I have "formed for Myself; they shall shew forth My praise" (Is.43: 21). Stephen, having made reference to the prophetic words of Moses in Deut. 18 proceeds to comment on his words by saying "This is He, that was in the Church in the wilderness" (Acts 7: 37, 38).

I believe that the foregoing gives to us some idea of the nature of "the Church of the living God" as it has existed throughout the ages. This of course is not to overlook, or in any way to detract from, the undeniable importance and significance of the great display of God's power on the Day of Pentecost. The events of that day were anticipated in the divine oracles of the Old Testament and were to have a crucial part to play in the outworking of God's glorious purposes of grace from that time to the end of the world. It is indeed necessary to distinguish between the form of the Church, as visibly displayed, under the Old Testament and its form under the New. Such a distinction is implied in the words of our Lord to Peter in Matt.16: 18 — "upon this rock I will build My Church". Jesus was there referring to the new form which the Church was to assume in consequence of His own Messianic work. He calls it "My Church". The greatest significance is to be attached to the new form of structure and administration established by the death, resurrection and ascension of Christ, and the outpouring of the Holy Spirit on the Day of Pentecost.

All I insist on here is that Pentecost did not mark the beginning of the existence of the Church, although it did mark the beginning of the functioning of the Church in its unique New Testament form. However, it is necessary for us to retain in our conception of the Church, its truly timeless character, and the timeless character of its Foundation. Abraham stands on the same Foundation as the apostle Paul. We are creatures of time, and naturally think consecutively. But not so God. The Church's unique Foundation is referred to by the apostle Peter in 1 Pet. 1:19–21. He "was foreordained before (and even 'slain from' [Rev.13:8]) the foundation of the world, but was manifest in these last times for" the Church.

VISIBLE AND INVISIBLE ASPECTS OF THE CHURCH

Next I propose to examine the visible and invisible aspects of the Church. The matter to be considered can perhaps best be identified by asking a question. Would it be correct to say that there is an invisible Church as well as a visible Church? The Church universal is comprised of men, women, boys and girls; called by God the Father into the fellowship of His Son, sanctified in Jesus Christ, regenerated by His Spirit, and united in the faith and confession of Christ Jesus as Lord and Saviour. It includes all people to whom the above definition is applicable, and who have ever lived. Many of whom being already in heaven.

Now it is true to say that there are aspects of the Church which are invisible. The actions of God by which individual people are made members of the mystical body of Christ are not discernible to men. The action of regeneration for instance is completely hidden from man, although the fruits of that action are discernible.

No man, or organisation of men, is able infallibly to determine who are regenerate and who are not, who are true believers and who are not. There are no visible marks which could *infallibly* settle this matter. If we reflect upon this subject we will see how impossible it would be for man to define the limits of the universal Church at any point in time. Apart from the impossibility of having an accurate computation of the Church in all corners of the earth, God is constantly adding "to the Church . . . such as should be saved" (Acts 2:47). For these reasons, if for no others, we must recognise the fact that there is an aspect of invisibility associated with the concept of the Church.

But the question to be faced is this. Are we, on these grounds, to conclude that there is such an entity as an invisible Church. This is so far from being just an academic matter that a wrong understanding of it is something that can have a detrimental effect on the life of the Church.

Every sincere Christian must face up to the fact that we are witnessing to-day a lamentable decline from the truth of the Gospel, viewed as the whole counsel of God, within the bounds of the Protestant denominations. Under these circumstances there is a danger that we comfort ourselves with the thought that we really belong to the "invisible" Church and that all our troubles and backslidings, and schisms, and party strifes are associated with the "visible" Church and that *that* will never be improved. Whereas on the other hand the "invisible" Church, it may be said, being entirely made up of "born-again" people, is the place where alone true fellowship and true unity can be found.

This is a comforting notion, and a convenient means of escape from the obligation to resolve the problems, and discouraging conditions, which often exist within local congregations. We must examine this point therefore, so that it may be determined whether we are entitled to make this distinction between the "visible" Church and the "invisible" Church. Or put in another way, and perhaps more specifically; when we think of the "visible" Church do we think of it in terms of a local church whereas when we think of the "invisible" Church do we think of it more in universal terms?

Our approach to this question must take account of the fact that every one who is a member of the organisation of the local church, which is visible and known to man, is not, on account of that, *necessarily* united to Christ by regeneration and faith. This concession is absolutely vital in considering the matter before us. The Church is constituted by a relation to Christ, which in itself is spiritual and invisible, and nothing *observable by men* can be the absolute and final criterion of that relation. A man can be *fairly* certain (using the means of discernment available to him) but never *absolutely* certain as to whether or not any particular person is a member of the body of Christ. Here is clearly recognised an invisible aspect of the Church.

We have a very striking illustration of this principle in John's Gospel account, chapter 15, verses 1 to 8. There the Lord Jesus Christ is depicting the Church in terms of Himself, in the guise of a vine with various branches. Some branches are living in the vine and draw the life-giving sap from the vine, and produce fruit. A perfect illustration of the Church, and compares with the illustration used by the apostle Paul of the human body, having many members, representing Christians drawn from all sections of society: Jews, Gentiles, bond and free. But in John 15 our Lord introduces this additional truth that in the Church, as manifest in this world, there will be some church members who appear to be much the same as the true members; having the appearance of branches, complying with expected standards of moral discipline, and giving a satisfactory formal profession of true religion; but not being vitally united to the vine, are not able to bring forth fruit.

But notwithstanding all that, we have no grounds for saying that the Church is an invisible entity divorced from its visible aspects. If there *were* such an entity as an "invisible" Church we would expect to find it in the New Testament, but it is nowhere to be found, but only invisible aspects of the Church. For instance, in the case of the Ephesian church, it is clearly a visible assembly of the saints. Human beings, who still had the defiling principle of sin in their hearts, notwithstanding the fact that they had been saved by grace through faith. It was this residue of sin in their hearts which made it necessary for Paul to stir up their spirits and to exhort them to holiness of life. Exhorting them to forbear one another; to endeavour to keep the unity of the Spirit; to speak every man truth with his neighbour; and so on; Paul called these people "saints" — but they were flesh and blood sinners as well (Eph.4:2, 3, 25).

All the churches referred to in the Acts of the Apostles and the Epistles were visible churches. For instance Paul refers in Romans 16: 4 to "all the churches of the Gentiles" and in verse 5 to the church that is in the house of Priscilla and Aquila. We see that the "Church" is always a visible observable entity. Union with Christ and the faith through which that union is effected, and the union of believers with one another in the body of Christ, are realities (though invisible) which find expression in what is observable.

The Church is Christ's Church. It is established and preserved by Him; and its continuance as an entity to be administered in accordance with His institution, is guaranteed by the fact that He is Head over all things to His body the Church (Eph.1:22).

Let us look, in this connection, at the statement which I made above, namely, that every one who has a place in the organisation of the Church which is visible and known to men, is not, on account of that, necessarily united to Christ by regeneration and faith.

The government and discipline in Christ's Church are exercised by men, in accordance with Christ's appointment, as discovered in His Word. Now we are obliged to recognise the fact that fallible men, though God's redeemed people, are not omniscient. *But Christ knows this.* What arrangements did He make, under such circumstances, for the proper administration of His Church? It is the responsibility of fallible men to decide who should be included, and who should be excluded, in respect of those applying for admission to a church.

THE MATTER OF GUIDANCE.

Clearly we are confronted here with the subject of guidance. There are many promises contained in the Scriptures in which God has promised to direct the ways of His people; and it is to God alone, and to the means which He has ordained, that we must always resort for guidance through the many dark passages of this earthly life. And there is no doubt that God hears the urgent cries of His people for such guidance. However we must never consequently conclude that we shall never take a wrong step. This of course is not due to any inadequacy of God's guiding grace but is entirely due to the fact that He is dealing with people who are still tainted with sin and who are therefore fallible.

What are the criteria then by which men are to judge and discriminate in this matter? What are the terms prescribed by the great Head of the Church? The determining factor is faith. "Then Simon himself believed also: and when he was baptised, he continued with Philip" — (Acts 8:13). "I believe that Jesus Christ is the Son of God" (Acts 8: 37). This professed faith however, did not have any automatic way of making its reality known, and consequently it could become effective in gaining visible admission to the Church, even when it is a false confession. This then was the criterion determining admission. However, confession alone, contradicted by conduct, could not be accepted as ground for admission. We may therefore define the acceptable grounds for admission as *an intelligent and consistent profession of faith in Christ accompanied by evident obedience to Him.* It is *not* the prerogative of man to search the heart of another, but it *is* his prerogative to judge, using the appropriate criteria in reference to public confession. The church officer *cannot,* and *must not* endeavour to, go beyond these criteria.

Now this limit of man's prerogative, and his inability to search the heart, is by divine appointment and institution. It is in this way that the Church, as a visible entity, administered by men in accordance with Christ's appointment, must admit to its fellowship those who make a credible profession of faith in Christ and promise obedience to Him. These grounds are evidently of such a nature that those who do not *have* true faith *may* declare them to the satisfaction of those responsible for their admission to a local church. In this way we see that we are faced with the anomaly that the visible entity which is called the church, *may* comprise within its membership those who do not really and truly belong to the body of Christ.

This same combination of the true and the false is found in the Church in the Old Testament economy. Some examples will evidence the reality of this phenomenon. God, speaking through Isaiah says "I have nourished and brought up children, and they have rebelled against Me" (Is.1: 2). Then in the next verse God owns them as His people — "Israel doth not know, My people doth not consider". They were His people by their Covenant relationship but by their conduct they had shown themselves not to be His *true* people. Paul wrote significantly in this respect — "he is not a Jew, which is one outwardly"; — (that is by the outward seal and sign of circumcision) — "neither is that circumcision, which is outward in the flesh: but he is a Jew, which is one inwardly; and circumcision is that of the heart" (Rom.2: 28, 29.). In Deut.32: 19, 20 God is speaking to His Covenant people (He calls them "sons"). "He abhorred them, because of the provoking of His sons" — "children in whom is no faith". Children who have broken the Covenant.

Referring to the nation of Israel, Thomas Shepard writes:— "God never took any to be His Church but as they were believers, at least externally, in that nation. I say believers; which either are *professed* believers, or *promised* believers, such as by outward Covenant shall have the means to be made believers in that nation; and hence you have heard that the nation of the Jews stood by faith, and were broken off by unbelief; and if any rejected the Covenant, as Ishmael and Esau, they were not of that Church, though they did and might dwell in that nation, as doubtless thousands did."

The teaching of the Scriptures is so clear and unmistakable on this point, that we are obliged to include it in our concept of the Church. What Paul is saying in Rom.2: 28, 29 could not be misunderstood. God had ordained the sign and seal of circumcision to *differentiate* those who had saving faith in Him, together with their household, and those who had not. God referred to them as *His people*. Circumcision was not intended by God to be a badge to differentiate the Jew from the Gentile, but it degenerated to the position in which it assumed that significance. On account of this, the apostle Paul anticipated a possible objection when, writing to the church at Rome he said ''What advantage then hath the Jew? or what profit is there of circumcision?'' — if it is not an infallible mark of the true people of God. Then he answered his own question — ''Much every way: chiefly, because that unto them were committed the oracles of God.'' (The Scriptures). We might equally well apply this to the Church in the Christian era — ''What advantage then has the Church? or what profit is there of baptism?'' — if it is not an infallible mark of the true people of God. The same reply can be given — ''Much every way — chiefly because that unto them were committed the oracles of God'' (Rom.3:1, 2).

In a unique way the Church has been given the custody of the Word of God. He has ''committed unto us the Word of reconciliation'' (2 Cor.5:19). ''The Church of the living God (is) the pillar and ground of the truth'' (1 Tim.3:15). It is no good the world looking anywhere else for ''the truth''.

SIGNIFICANCE OF CIRCUMCISION

The true significance of circumcision is clearly stated by the apostle Paul, again in this epistle to the Romans — Abraham ''received the sign of circumcision, a seal of the righteousness of *the faith which he had* being yet uncircumcised'' (Rom.4: 11). Similarly we could say in this Christian era, concerning an adult man who had confessed faith in the Lord Jesus Christ (being of course equally true of a woman), that he received the sign of baptism, a seal of the righteousness of the faith which he had being yet unbaptised. And yet in both cases not *all* who have received the sign and seal of the Covenant; whether it be circumcision or baptism; are necessarily the true people of God. John the Baptist said to some of the leading Jews of his day ''think not to say within yourselves, We have Abraham to our father: for I say unto you, that God is able of these stones to raise up children unto Abraham'' (Matt.3: 9). Our Lord said, ''Many shall come from the east and west, and shall sit down with Abraham, and Isaac, and Jacob, in the kingdom of heaven. But the children of the kingdom (some of the visible members of the Church) shall be cast out into outer darkness: there shall be weeping and gnashing of teeth'' (Matt.8: 11, 12).

We cannot leave this particular aspect of our subject without noticing those moving heartfelt and pathetic sentiments expressed by the apostle Paul (himself a Jew) for his fellow countrymen, realising that many of them were not the true people of God: ''I have great heaviness and continual sorrow in my heart. For I could wish that myself were accursed from Christ for my brethren, my kinsmen according to the flesh: who are Israelites; to whom pertaineth the adoption, and the glory, and the covenants, and the giving of the law, and the service of God, and the promises; — not as though the Word of God hath taken none effect. For they are not all Israel, which are of Israel: neither, because they are the seed of Abraham, are they all children; but, in Isaac shall thy seed be called. That is, They which are the children of the flesh, these are not the children of God: but the children of the promise are counted for the seed.'' (vv.2, 3, 4, 6, 7, 8 of Rom.9). Not ''all Israel'' (the true people of God) ''which are of Israel'' (the people of God by outward Covenant). In this way God is insisting that His people must never recline in a state of false security (as the Pharisees did) on the fact of having received the sign and seal of the Covenant, but rather that they must ever, as in the words of the apostle Peter, '' — give diligence to make your calling and election sure'' (2 Pet. 1:10).

As we have seen, the very administration which Christ has instituted for the admission of members into the Church allows for the admission of hypocrites. However we must not allow *this* fact to modify our description of the Church as comprising those who ''are sanctified in Christ Jesus, called to be saints'', as Paul describes the Corinthian church, in spite of the fact that in chapter 5 of his first epistle to them he shows that there were those found in their midst who were guilty of gross sin, and were to be excluded from their fellowship. The ultimate definition of the Church, notwithstanding all its blemishes and misjudgments, is this. It is the complete number of those whom the Father has given to the Son and who have been united to Christ by the sovereign and irresistible power of the Holy Spirit (see 1 Cor.12: 13).

The ultimate concept of the glorified Church is of '' — a great multitude, which no man could number, of all nations, and kindreds, and people, and tongues, — clothed with white robes — washed — in the blood of the Lamb'' (see Rev.7: 9 and 14). A company of people which will never again be mingled with unbelievers, for ''there shall in no wise enter into it any thing that defileth, neither whatsoever worketh abomination, or maketh a lie: but they which are written in the Lamb's book of life'' (Rev. 21: 27).

From the foregoing we must conclude that the Church as it exists on earth is essentially visible, because it is comprised of visible people who are governed by visible organisations and relationships, and who manifest visible gifts and admit visible responsibilities.

ESSENTIAL UNITY OF CHURCH

We have noticed that there is an essential unity in the Church as seen in the *Old* Testament economy. They were God's Covenant people, and there were no sub-divisions of this body of people. It remains for us finally, under this section, to examine the nature of the Church in the *New* Testament economy, in order to determine whether there is here a corresponding unity.

When Jesus was speaking to Peter He said ''upon this rock I will build my Church'' (Matt.16: 18). The expression ''My Church'' refers to the Church universal; those gathered and knit together after the pattern provided by the Old Testament, as a community which stands in a relation to Him, comparable to the congregation of the Lord in the Old Testament. The other occasion (and there were only two) on which Jesus referred to the Church, is found in Matt.18: 17 where He is giving instructions regarding Church discipline. Here He says ''tell it unto the church''. On this occasion Jesus is referring to a local church, being the place where particular discipline is exercised. Taking these two occasions together we find that Jesus taught that there was such an entity as a local church, whilst at the same time establishing the fact that the Church could be considered as an entity of universal extent. The same Greek word EKKLESIA was used for both the universal Church and the local church.

Many other references to particular local churches are found in the Acts of the Apostles and in Paul's epistles. Examples of these are as follows: "the church which was at Jerusalem" (Acts 8: 1 & 11:22). The church at Antioch (Acts 14: 27). "The church which is at Cenchrea" (Rom.16: 1), and many others. Also we find references to various local churches in certain areas, for instance; the churches in Syria and Cilicia (Acts 15: 41) and "the churches of Galatia" (1 Cor.16: 1 and Gal.1: 2), Paul even speaks of the church in a house (Rom.16: 5; 1 Cor.16: 19).

As Jesus used the word "church" in both senses, that is, as representing a local church and as representing the Church universal, so does Paul. Paul said "I persecuted the Church of God" (1 Cor.15: 9), i.e. the universal Church. The universal aspect of the Church appears also in 1 Cor.10: 32 — "Give none offence, neither to the Jews, nor to the Gentiles, nor to the Church of God." There are several other Scriptures which bring out the universal nature of the Church, but these examples will satisfy our present purpose.

How then do we reconcile these two aspects of the Church as spoken of in the New Testament? The local church is a recognised and accepted entity in the eyes of the Lord Jesus Christ, and so is the Church universal.

The sheer logic of the matter, and the unavoidable restrictions arising from the world-wide extent of the Church, render it impossible for all the people of God to gather themselves together under one roof. The universal Church must be sub-divided into a multitude of localities, and the people of God in each locality gather together in one building (it may even be a private house) in order to function as a local church, in corporate worship, in declaring the whole counsel of God, in administering the sacraments, in exercising spiritual gifts for the mutual benefit of all, in ordering right government, and in any other exercises proper to the Church as prescribed in the Scriptures.

Each local church is an integral part of the Church universal and is answerable alone to the great Head of the Church. It is when we consider the Church as being the body of Christ that its unity and its true ecumenical character is appreciated. This aspect is recognised in Paul's salutation to "the church of God which is at Corinth, . . . with all that in every place call upon the name of Jesus

Christ our Lord, both theirs and ours'' (1 Cor. 1:2). ''There is one body, and one Spirit, even as ye are called in one hope of your calling; one Lord, one faith, one baptism, one God and Father of all, who is above all, and through all, and in you all'' (Eph.4: 4–6). In that great high priestly prayer Jesus prayed to the Father — ''Neither pray I for these alone, but for them also which shall believe on Me through their word; that they all may be one; as Thou, Father, art in Me, and I in Thee, that they also may be one in Us'' (John 17: 20, 21).

The lack of true unity within and among the churches of Christ is a violation of the essential unity of the body of Christ. We cannot escape from our obligations in this respect by resorting to the notion of the ''invisibile'' Church. The unity for which Jesus prayed must be a visible unity because it was directed to the end ''that the world may believe'' (John 17:21).

To sum up this general consideration of the Church universal we conclude that the Church is a visible entity possessing several invisible characteristics. It fulfils a vital role in the whole economy of God in the publishing of His purposes of grace to this sinful fallen and corrupted human race. It existed in embryo form at the very dawn of history, and has continued in existence, and expanded, down through the running centuries to this present day. At Pentecost the Church assumed a new form of structure and administration, whilst still retaining its essential character, as comprising, as it ever did, ''all that in every place call upon the name of Jesus Christ our Lord . . .'' (l Cor. 1: 2). The Church universal is generically one. ''. . . the God and Father of our Lord Jesus Christ .. gave Him to be the Head over all things to the Church, which is His body, the fulness of Him that filleth all in all'' (Eph.1: 3, 22, 23).

In view of the fact that God has in this way declared His purpose through His united Church, any ecclesiastical distinctions, systems or organisations, which introduce unwarranted differences which mitigate against this declared purpose of God, should be recognised as being detrimental and inimical to God's great plan of redemption, and consequently to be the subject of the urgent cries and pleadings of God's people. God tells us through His prophet Isaiah what provision He has made for His Church. But He will not have us leave it at that. God requires something of *us* — He looks for those who are called "the Lord's remembrancers" ("ye that make mention of the LORD") — those within the Church who will exercise industriously, day and night, their ministry of praying and teaching and warning the people. "I have set watchmen upon thy walls, O Jerusalem (the Church), which shall never hold their peace day nor night: ye that make mention of the LORD, keep not silence, and give Him no rest, till He establish, and till He make Jerusalem a praise in the earth" (Is.62: 6, 7).

Do we need any *further* convincing as to why God's people should in this way cry out to the God of heaven for the peace and prosperity of the Church (Ps.122: 6, 7)? and why those should be put to shame who do not exert all their energies to this end? Well, then, here is the *ultimate* reason, here is the argument that silences *all* arguments: "Christ-loved the Church, and gave Himself for it; that He might sanctify and cleanse it with the washing of water by the Word, that He might present it to Himself a glorious Church, not having spot, or wrinkle, or any such thing; but that it should be holy and without blemish" (Eph.5: 25–27). If *that* is the Lord Christ's objective in giving Himself for His Church, then it should also be the objective of every member of His mystical body, reaching over and through all hindrances, and casting down all barriers that lie in the way of it.

★ ★ ★

"He hath made with me an everlasting Covenant, ordered in all things, and sure: for this is all my salvation, and all my desire."

2 Sam.23:5.

THE COVENANT OF GRACE

Let us pause briefly at this point before we cross the threshold into the treasure house of God's matchless grace, and endeavour to see this Covenant in its proper setting, and see ourselves as participants and legatees of the agreement between our beneficent God and unworthy guilty sinners — creatures of the dust.

See how the Puritan Richard Alleine proclaims the introduction of this Covenant with (as it were) the sound of trumpets!

> "Good news from heaven! ... God hath made and established a new Covenant ... This Covenant is the hope of sinners; the riches of saints; the Magna Charta of the city of God; the forfeited lease of eternity renewed; God's ... gift wherein He hath, on fair conditions, granted sinners their lives, and settled upon His saints an everlasting inheritance."

The word "covenant" is found in the Old Testament and New Testament Scriptures, whereas the word "testament", which carries a very similar meaning, and is a translation of the same Greek word which stands for "covenant", is found only in the New Testament. Both words represent a special arrangement made by God in conjunction with man, incorporating conditions and contingent punishments or blessings.

It is generally understood that there are two covenants between God and men represented in the Scriptures, one referred to as "The Covenant of Works", which God entered into with Adam, and the other referred to as "The Covenant of Grace" which God entered into with His chosen people. The governing feature of the former, being the performance of works, and that of the latter, being the bestowal of grace. It could be objected that the former is not referred to in the Scriptures as a covenant, although some take it that Hosea 6:7 is a reference to it. ''— like men'' can very properly be translated ''like Adam'' so referring to Adam's breaking the Covenant of Works. Quite apart from this, however, the arrangement which God made with Adam is so well suited to the term ''covenant'' and bears all the marks of a covenant, that it has been found to be a convenient term to use to describe the situation and the relationship which existed between the Creator and the man which He had created in His own image. This ''Covenant of Works'' should not be confused with what is referred to as the ''old covenant'' or the ''first covenant'' in, for instance, Heb.8: 7 & 13.

''The Covenant of Works'' was unique and was not redemptive, but the Mosaic covenant, so called, to which reference will be made later, *was* redemptive. The ''Covenant of Works'' refers only to the arrangement made by God with Adam in his state of innocence before the Fall, and therefore applies to Adam alone, as the federal head of the human race. It was not a covenant in the sense that man was at liberty to decline its terms, but rather he was under an obligation to accept whatever terms God might choose to impose. The condition of the Covenant was obedience. Adam disobeyed, and consequently the Covenant was broken, and so he was immediately subjected to the previously prescribed *punishments* of God, instead of His *blessings.*

Although this Covenant was unique in that it referred essentially to Adam alone, nevertheless one of the characteristics of the ''Covenant of Works'' was that Adam, as already mentioned, was being considered as a *public* person and not just a *private* person. Under this Covenant *one* stood for *all*. Adam was the federal head and representative of all that were to be descended from him. The whole human race, until the end of the world, was on trial in him. As *he* failed, the whole of mankind failed with him, in his immensely significant transgression. The aspect of truth lying behind this principle is what is often referred to as ''Covenant Theology'', which teaches that God always deals with man on the basis of a covenant and He always has someone to represent man. Adam was man's representative in the Covenant of Works. Man's representative in the Covenant of Grace was the last Adam, Christ (l Cor.15: 45). This principle lies at the root of that most vital branch of the Christian religion, namely the doctrine of justification *by faith only*, so cogently reasoned out by Paul in Rom.5: 12–21. As Adam was the federal head and representative of the whole human race, the punishments inflicted upon him have consequently and automatically been inflicted on all mankind, summed up in the one word "death" (Gen.2: 17).

As the Covenant of Works was broken on man's part, the relationship between God and man could have been declared null and void, and the whole human race arising out of the loins of Adam, whom he represented, abandoned to eternal ruin. However God had a plan for this contingency, prepared before the foundation of the world, by which He made provision for the eternal redemption of a specific number of people, known only to Himself, and which He designed to call out of the world of fallen mankind, which was under sentence of death due to Adam's transgression. The terms of this plan, by which God purposed to redeem a people for Himself, constituted what has been referred to as "The Covenant of Grace".

Now it would, I think, enable us to obtain a clearer view of God's purpose of grace at this point, if we were to observe the steps, as it were, in the divine economy. We have seen how God, according to His own good pleasure, and His perfect and all-wise counsels, entered into an arrangement with Adam; which we have called "The Covenant of Works"; by the terms of which He promised certain blessings, and threatened certain punishments, which were contingent upon Adam's obedience; which Covenant was broken. No further covenant could be made with the defaulter, Adam, so the new covenant; "The Covenant of Grace", was entered into with Christ as the "second Man" (l Cor.15: 47), and with all believers mystically in Him. It was made with Him primarily, as the Head, (in the same way as the Covenant of Works was made primarily with Adam, as the head) and with the elect of God as members of His mystical body, who personally come into this Covenant when they come into union with Him by *faith*. So we can say that the Covenant of Grace is made with all believers, in Christ.

A person yet unborn but having his name "written in the Lamb's book of life" (Rev.21: 27), and so destined to be a party to the Covenant of Grace, may, when born into this world, walk for some time" according to the course of this world, according to the prince of the power of the air" (Eph.2: 2). And it is only when he is saved by grace "through faith" (Eph.2: 8) that he becomes an actual beneficiary under the terms of the Covenant. In other words, when he becomes a *believer*. The benefits of the Covenant are suspended on the condition of *believing*, and yet sovereignly and infallibly appointed by God on the sole ground of his election. It is in this sense that we say that the Covenant of Grace is made with all believers, in Christ.

Although it may appear to be an abstruse distinction, it is nevertheless a matter of great significance and importance that we insist on this detail relating to the Covenant of Grace. This Covenant was properly made *with every believer* as he is a member of Christ's mystical body. Consequently we must not say, as has been said by some, that those duties which are required by the Covenant, are required only to be performed by Christ. Rather they are required to be performed by *us* in His strength. Christ does not repent and believe for us, but *we* have to do these things, in the strength of His grace, otherwise we have no part in the blessings of the Covenant.

One further thing which must be observed in this connection is this. This Covenant of Grace, made with believers in Christ, must not be confused with what has often been referred to as "The Covenant of Redemption". The Covenant of Redemption was made within the Godhead with the eternal Son before the foundation of the world. It was made *for* us but not *with* us. Its conditions were laid on Christ alone, namely that He was to assume our nature and pour "out His soul unto death" (Is.53: 12), and all other requirements by means of which God purposed to redeem a people for Himself.

This is how Francis Turretin defined the Covenant of Grace:— "The Covenant of Grace is a gratuitous pact between God the offended one and man the offender, entered into in Christ, in which God freely, on account of Christ, promises to man the remission of sins and salvation, and man in dependence upon the same grace promises faith and obedience."

Ezekiel Culverwell declares that "faith is an impossible condition to be performed of ourselves" for it is itself "part of the thing promised" for in the Covenant of Grace God "freely promises not only life but also to give grace to *receive* this life".

The irreversible character of God's Covenant is underlined by the psalmist: "My Covenant will I not break, nor alter the thing that is gone out of My lips" (Ps.89: 34).

D. M. Lloyd-Jones, commenting on Rom. 4 says: "There is only one Covenant of Grace, and men in all dispensations are saved in exactly the same way. It is the same Covenant of Grace under the Old Testament as it is under the New. There is a difference of administration, but it is the same Covenant of Grace. There is only one way of salvation always, whether in the past, present or future". Then calling the apostle Paul's statement in Eph. ch.2 as "In many ways the classic statement" of this principle, he goes on to quote this statement "Ye who sometimes were afar off." — who were "aliens from the commonwealth of Israel, and strangers from the covenants of promise, having no hope, and without God in the world . . . are made nigh by the blood of Christ". "Ye are no more strangers and foreigners, but fellow-citizens with the saints, (the Old Testament saints) and of the household of God". Finally Lloyd-Jones remarks "Let us never forget this. We Gentiles are simply brought into that which was already in existence. It is not something entirely new. The Jews were in it before; we are brought into it with them. We are fellow-heirs with them, fellow possessors, fellow citizens."

The apostle writing to the Hebrews (Ch.11 v.39) tells us that the Old Testament saints "obtained a good report through faith". (In the same way as is open to New Testament saints).

John Brown expounding the following verse (v.40) says "God has so arranged matters, that the complete accomplishment of the promise (contained in the Covenant), both to the Old Testament and New Testament believers, shall take place together. They shall be made perfect but not without us; we and they shall attain perfection together." (In the heavenly state). [Author's parentheses].

GENERAL CONSIDERATION

We will now consider this Covenant of Grace rather more generally, and observe the vital role that it has to play in all God's subsequent dealings with mankind. It would I think be helpful in this respect to restate some of the critical issues which we have looked at so far, in order to have them rather more prominently before our mind's eye.

God created man in His own image, perfect, upright, sinless, and placed him in the perfect environment of the Garden of Eden; and He created woman to be his companion. He made an agreement with Adam, the Covenant of Works, incorporating certain conditions. On God's side there were implied conditions of blessings, and on Adam's side there was the condition of obedience, together with the understanding that Adam was standing federally for the whole human race. Adam sinned by disobeying God's command, and so broke the Covenant, as a direct result of which the whole human race, from Adam onwards, was plunged into misery under judgment of death.

God the Son, in covenant with God the Father, and in conjunction with God the Spirit, undertook the redemption of fallen man, in accordance with a plan of redemption designed by the Father. A specific number of people were chosen by the Father, before the foundation of the world, to be those who should benefit from this plan, whose names were then written in the Lamb's book of life. These names were one of "the secret things" belonging to the Lord our God (see Deut.29: 29).

According to the terms of the Covenant of Redemption, God the Father placed in the care of God the Son all this company of His chosen people whose names were written in the book. John 6:37 — "All that the Father giveth Me shall come to Me; and him that cometh to Me I will in no wise cast out." At the same time, and under the terms of the same Covenant, the Father gave power to the Son as the Mediator (He already possessed all power as God the Son) to give eternal life to each one of them (Jn. 17:2). This was a specific task undertaken, and accomplished. "I have manifested Thy name unto the men which Thou gavest Me out of the world: Thine they were, and Thou gavest them Me; and they have kept Thy word" (Jn.17: 6).

The names of this favoured company of people have been kept secret ever since. No one would have suspected that the thief on the cross was one of them. Certainly *they are not known to anyone* until one by one they receive God's irresistible call — (see Rom.8: 28–30) — and for this reason the Gospel must be preached to *all*. No man knows who are the elect of God until the elect are born again, and even after they have been born again the visible signs of the new life are often fainter than they ought to be.

Because of the remains of sin in the human heart there is sometimes a degree of uncertainty in the minds of individuals, even after a person has been born again, as to whether or not they belong to that favoured number. But by God's grace, and for our comfort, He has provided various means of obtaining assurance regarding this most vital matter, which we will now consider briefly.

There appear to be three main grounds of assurance which I will mention in ascending order. *First* of *all* assurance may be obtained from the Word of God itself. For instance, as we read John 3: 36 — "He that believeth on the Son *hath* everlasting life", we say to ourselves that it is God who is saying that, and therefore it *must* be true. I believe on the Son of God and therefore I *must* have everlasting life. That is *one* means of obtaining assurance. *Secondly,* assurance may be obtained by observing whether certain signs of the new life are evident. John in his first epistle speaks of some of these, such as: (a) Believing that Jesus is the Christ. (b) Loving the brethren. (c) Keeping God's commandments. (d) Having the Spirit of God. There are various indications as to whether we *have* the Spirit of God dwelling in us, such as (i) Having a desire for more knowledge of the Scriptures. (ii) An increasing sensitivity to sin. (iii) Bringing forth fruits of the Spirit. *Finally,* assurance may be obtained by the Spirit bearing "witness with our spirit, that we are the children of God" (Rom.8: 16). This is a subjective, invisible, assurance. A sort of inner intuition. The sort of thing referred to in Rev.2: 17 — the white stone with a new name written.

John Murray, referring to the need for assurance says this:— "It is not sufficient that members of the Church should be true believers and be heirs of eternal life. (He means unassuredly so.) It is also necessary that they be self-consciously and intelligently so. The apostles were aware of this need in their day. 'These things have I written unto you that believe on the name of the Son of God; that ye may know that ye have eternal life' (1 John 5: 13). 'Wherefore the rather, brethren, give diligence to make your calling and election sure; for if ye do these things, ye shall never fall' (2 Pet.1: 10). The low ethical and spiritual plane on which true Christians often live, finds its explanation in the failure to bring within explicit consciousness the status that belongs to them by God's grace in Christ, and the hope of the promise in the Gospel.''

Well I have spent time on this point in order to emphasise the secret character of the identity of those to whom God has given the gift of eternal life. Individuals do not know that they are among this number *before* they are regenerated. Even *after* regeneration some lack assurance of their position. Furthermore, it may not always be clear to others whether a person is regenerate or not, although God has provided a means of recognition by the fruits produced in their lives.

As mentioned before there is a specific number of people whose names are written in the Lamb's book of life, and *that* number is fixed for all eternity, and the Covenant of Grace relates to those people alone. However, it is important to observe that although in the counsel of God all His chosen people were known to Him by name, in eternity, before the foundation of the world, and as such, already have the invisible seal of the Covenant upon them. Although that is so, nevertheless, they are only brought to a personal discovery of this their privileged position at some point in time. In this way, and with this understanding, it may be said that these people enter into the Covenant one by one, at various points in time, and there is only one entrance ticket, as it were, and that is *faith*. It was *always* by faith, and by faith alone, from the very first person to enter into the Covenant at the very dawn of history, down to the present day. The fact that a person is not a party to the Covenant until faith has been exercised is brought out strikingly, in Paul's epistle to the Ephesians, chapter 2. Even the elect and chosen people of God are described as ''dead in trespasses and sins . . .'' The change came when God quickened them; created within them a new principle of life. The change enabled them to believe on the Mediator of the Covenant (Eph.2: 1, 2, 8; Heb.9: 15)

In this way the Church was gradually formed, as individuals were called out of the fallen corrupt world. We could look upon the total number of God's elect people as represented by the capacity of a large vessel, and as God calls His people out of the world He puts them into this vessel, and over the centuries and millenia the vessel has been filling up. This process will go on with the Lord adding to the Church until the vessel is full and the Church is complete and all God's people are gathered in.

From the beginning of time the Church has comprised individual people whom God effectually called out of the total population of the unbelieving world from generation to generation, and it was on the basis of the Covenant of Grace, and the promises associated with that Covenant, that each individual, thus called, was entitled to be, and was indeed, added to the Church.

The promise of God which summarises the principle on which the Church is constituted, and which is the essence of the terms of God's undertaking in the Covenant, is "I will be their God, and they shall be My people" (Jer.31: 33). This is the promise of grace upon which rests the communion of the people of God in all ages. It applies to the New Testament period as well as the Old Testament period. The Covenant was sealed with the blood of Christ. It is called a "new testament" but it is the same Covenant of Grace republished with clearer significance (see Luke 22: 20).

The following is what the Westminster Confession of Faith says about this Covenant:—

> "This Covenant was differently administered in the time of the Law, and in the time of the Gospel: under the Law it was administered by promises, prophecies, sacrifices, circumcision, the paschal lamb, and other types and ordinances delivered to the people of the Jews, all fore-signifying Christ to come, which were for that time sufficient and efficacious, through the operation of the Spirit, to instruct and build up the elect in faith in the promised Messiah, by whom they had full remission of sins, and eternal salvation; and is called the Old Testament."

> "Under the Gospel, when Christ the substance was exhibited, the ordinances in which this Covenant is

> dispensed are the preaching of the Word, and the administration of the sacraments of Baptism and the Lord's Supper; which, though fewer in number, and administered with more simplicity and less outward glory, yet in them it is held forth in more fulness, evidence, and spiritual efficacy, to all nations, both Jews and Gentiles; and is called the New Testament. There are not therefore two covenants of grace differing in substance, but one and the same under various dispensations."

In the same way as something was required of man in the Covenant of Works in order to qualify for the benefits and promises of God promulgated in the Covenant, which requirement (obedience) could properly be called a condition;so something was required of man under the Covenant of Grace, in order to qualify for *its* benefits, and again we will refer to this as a condition. The benefit of *this* Covenant, which is essentially that of salvation, is suspended until something is performed by the potential beneficiary. The thing that must be performed is the exercising of faith, for we read "He that believeth on the Son hath everlasting life: and he that believeth not the Son shall not see life; but the wrath of God abideth on him" (still) (John 3: 36). So the benefit of the Covenant is suspended, as it were, on believing; on faith. But as Paul tells us — "and *that* (faith) not of yourselves, it is the gift of God" (Eph.2: 8).

Although there is but one Covenant of Grace that governs God's dealings with mankind from the beginning to the end of time, it has had several publishings and different settings, and this aspect would seem to present itself next for our consideration.

The first significant point in the progress of the Church, after its inception, is at the time of Abraham. Previous to that time, as already observed, the Church was composed of those individuals who had been called by God out of the rest of the world's unbelieving population. God confirmed His Covenant of Grace at that time in terms of the promise given to Abraham. A very significant promise: "I will make of thee a great nation, and I will bless thee, and make thy name great; and thou shalt be a blessing: . . . in thee shall all families of the earth be blessed" (Gen.12: 2, 3). This promise reaches out to the end of time. William Perkins said in this connection, "In the person of Abraham, God ... hath made Covenant with *us*; and He hath sworn unto *us*. What can we more require of Him? What better ground of true comfort?".

When we come to consider the signs and seals of the Covenant, we will be giving attention to the way that, as God received Abraham into the Church according to the terms of the Covenant, (for he believed God) so also He recognised Abraham's family, including his infant seed, as part of Abraham himself, and for his sake. It was a mark of God's grace and favour towards Abraham personally.

The Church in the New Testament, or Gospel, period is founded upon this Covenant made with Abraham; and the Church's administration, in this period of the New Testament, is the extension and unfolding of the Abrahamic Covenant, which was the confirmed Covenant of Grace. This is seen in Paul's argument to the Galatians, particularly in chapter 3, verses 6 to 17. Faith is the governing principle, the condition, on man's part, of the Covenant of Grace. Abraham believed, and it was accounted (or imputed) to him for righteousness. (See also Rom.4: 5, 6). New Testament believers of all nations, Jews and Gentiles, are Abraham's seed and heirs according to the promise.

The next significant point in the progress of the Church, *after* the time of Abraham, is at the time of the giving of the Law. It is important that we are clear about the significance of this stage, because much confusion has occurred in the Church on account of a wrong understanding of this phase of its development. In other words we should consider the question as to what was God's purpose in publishing the Law. Was it legal or evangelical? Or to use Paul's wording: "Wherefore then serveth the law" and he answers his own question "It was *added* because of transgressions" (Gal.3: 19). In other words the Law was a sort of appendix added to the Covenant of Grace to highlight the nature and potency of sin. Man had become slack, and his sense of sin had been blunted, so God gave clear outlines by means of the Law, to delineate His own true character as well as the true character of sin. Paul confessed: "I had not known lust, except the law had said, Thou shalt not covet" (Rom. 7:7). But in Galatians Paul tells us that this arrangement was intended by God "to bring us unto Christ" (Gal.3: 24). Clearly the intent of the Law was evangelical and not legal. In other words the Law did not disannul the Covenant — (Gal.3:17): "And this I say, that the Covenant, that was confirmed before of God in Christ, the law, which was four hundred and thirty years after, cannot disannul, that it should make the promise of none effect."

The next significant point in the progress of the Church, and the most significant of all, was the first advent of the Lord Jesus Christ, with which we should join the advent of the Spirit on the Day of Pentecost. The imminent visible entry of Christ onto the stage of this world is dramatically foretold by Malachi, the last of the prophets of the Old Testament, in these thrilling words to His expectant people: "The Lord, whom ye seek, shall suddenly come to His temple, even the Messenger of the Covenant, whom ye delight in: behold, He shall come, saith the LORD of Hosts." (Mal. 3:1). God said through Jeremiah: "I will make an everlasting Covenant with them" (Jer.32: 40). And the promise of the Covenant is the same, in essence, as before: " . . . they shall be My people, and I will be their God" (Jer.32: 38). And again: " . . . let us join ourselves to the LORD in a perpetual Covenant that shall not be forgotton" (Jer.50: 5). "My kindness shall not depart from thee, neither shall the Covenant of My peace be removed, saith the LORD that hath mercy upon thee" (Is.54: 10). Also: "My Covenant will I not break, nor alter the thing that is gone out of my lips" (Ps.89: 34). These Scriptures are linked to, and reflected in, what we find in Heb.13: 20: "the blood of the everlasting Covenant". In a word, Christ was sent to make good all the promises of the Covenant.

So we see that there is only one Covenant of Grace, and only one condition for participating in it, namely faith. Only one Saviour and only one salvation. A clear instance of how in the days of the apostles there were some who believed that the Law of Moses was a covenant of works appears in Acts chapter 15: verse 1" certain men taught the brethren, and said, Except ye be circumcised after the manner of Moses, ye cannot be saved." Peter then said: "Why tempt ye God, to put a yoke upon the neck of the disciples, which neither our fathers nor we were able to bear?" (verse 10). Thereby underlining the fact that no man can be justified by the Law. All the hope of the Old Testament saints, and ours, rests solely on the terms of the Covenant of Grace. And to confirm the fact that Old

Testament and New Testament saints are saved in exactly the same way Peter adds: "We believe that through the grace of the Lord Jesus Christ we shall be saved, even as they" (Acts 15: 11). Meaning we shall be saved in exactly the same way (even in minute particulars) as our fathers (including Abraham) were saved; namely by faith alone.

As observed earlier, the first glimmerings of the Covenant of Grace were comparatively weak and obscure, as it was first published in the Garden of Eden in the promise recorded in Gen.3: 15. This promise was like the first small spring at the head of a great river, which the further it runs the bigger it grows by the accession of more waters to it. God has in all ages been amplifying the privileges and heightening the glory of this Covenant of Grace in all the subsequent editions of it up to its fullest declaration in the person of the Lord Jesus Christ. Peter tells us that though the Paschal Lamb of God was hidden from former ages, He was manifest in these last times for those who had saving faith in Him, even before He was manifested (1 Pet.1:19–21). The Church in the Old Testament times was longing for this fuller revelation of the Covenant: the psalmist said: "My soul fainteth for Thy salvation" (Ps.119: 81). Isaiah wrote: "Lo, this is our God; we have waited for Him, and He will save us" (Is.25: 9). The aged Simeon, at the very threshold of the display of God's grace, said: "Mine eyes have seen Thy salvation, which Thou hast prepared before the face of all people" (Luke 2: 30, 31). The Covenant, first appearing in those early glimmerings, has thus in these latter days approached the clear shining of noonday, with the whole fallen creation groaning and travailing in pain, looking for that blessed hope, and the glorious appearing of the great God and our Saviour Jesus Christ. (see Rom.8: 22; Titus 2: 13).

I have just described the evolving character of the Covenant of Grace as "the first small spring at the head of a great river". The following is the way that the Puritan John Flavel expresses it – "Though the first glimmerings of this Covenant of Grace, were comparatively weak and obscure; yet from the first publication of it to Adam, God in all ages hath been amplifying the privileges, and heightening the glory of this Covenant in all the after editions of it unto this day, and will more and more amplify and illustrate it to the end of the world". (No doubt by "illustrate" Flavel intends the less common meaning – "make illustrious").

"Begotten again by the resurrection of Jesus Christ from the dead, to an inheritance incorruptible, and undefiled, and that fadeth not away, reserved in heaven."

1 Pet.1:3, 4.

"Tell me Thou art mine, O Saviour,
Grant me an assurance clear;
Banish all my dark misgivings,
Still my doubtings, calm my fear.
O, my soul within me yearneth
Now to hear Thy voice divine;
So shall grief be gone for ever
And despair no more be mine."

William Williams.

"How sweet and excellent soever the foretastes of heaven are, heaven itself will be an unspeakable surprise to the saints, when they shall come thither."

John Flavel.

THE SIGNS AND SEALS OF THE COVENANT OF GRACE

God, in His infinite wisdom, instituted certain signs and seals to be associated with the Covenant of Grace. However, in the period of time between Adam and Abraham no such token was ordained, but the reason for this is concealed from us, and we do not need to search for a reason, as it depends on God's secret counsel.

The introduction of the ''sign'', or ''token'', of circumcision at the time of Abraham is referred to in Gen.17:11 where we read — ''it (circumcision) shall be a token of the Covenant betwixt Me and you''. The word translated ''token'' stands for the ''sign'' of anything which cannot itself be seen. We should also notice how the apostle Paul refers to this Scripture in Rom.4:11 — ''And he (Abraham) received the sign of circumcision, a seal of the righteousness of the faith which he had yet being uncircumcised''. The word translated ''seal'' stands for that by which anything is confirmed, proved and authenticated. The word translated ''sign'' is equivalent to ''mark'' or ''token'', and stands for that by which a person is distinguished from others and known. The word is used in the same way in Matt.26:48, where we read how Judas Iscariot gave the chief priests and elders a ''sign'' to distinguish the One he was betraying. The ''sign'' in that case was a kiss. The word is used similarly in Luke 2:12, and also in 2 Thess.3:17 where Paul tells us how he writes his salutation with his own hand as a ''token'' or ''sign'' of the authenticity of the epistle. Rather as we are familiar with the practice of appending a literal seal and signature to a document to authenticate it and confirm it to be true and genuine. Which idea brings out the sense and application of the word very well as it is used in connection with the Covenant of Grace. So we are able to conclude that circumcision is a sign and a seal of the blessings held out by God to His people in the Covenant of Grace, as also is baptism.

The fact that is clearly placed before us in the Scriptures is that when God called out a *nation* for Himself, in the person of Abraham, He also instituted the rite of circumcision as a sign and a seal of the Covenant. At the same time He renewed His Covenant in these words: ''This is My Covenant, which ye shall keep, between Me and you and thy seed after thee''. Then God recites the terms of the Covenant: ''Every man child among you shall be circumcised . . . and it shall be a token of the Covenant betwixt Me and you''. Then follow detailed instructions regarding who should be the subjects of circumcision, which include his infant seed (Gen.17: 10–14. See also Acts 7:8 and Rom.4:11)

This fact then is beyond any dispute, that the Covenant, renewed and enlarged with Abraham, included his infant offspring. In other words, from this we see that the Church at that time included not only those adults who confessed the true religion but also their infant seed. Which point has already been enlarged upon when considering the nature of the Covenant itself. Probably the most important point to be observed here, is the fact that the rite of circumcision was administered to the infant seed of believing parents *by divine command*. It is good that we consider the implications of this, but whatever conclusion we may arrive at in this respect, that fact remains, that it was *a divine command*, and the sign of circumcision thus administered was the divinely appointed sign of the Covenant.

Circumcision consisted (as all sacraments do) of an external sign, and a spiritual mystery signified thereby. The external sign, was the cutting off of the foreskin of the males. The spiritual mystery, thereby signified and represented, was the severing of the filth and guilt of sin from their souls by regeneration and justification, called ''the circumcision of the heart'' in Deut. 10: 16.

It is important that we have a clear view of the deep spiritual significance of the token of circumcision. We must not say that circumcision was simply the sign of an external relationship, or merely a sign of national identity. It is true that the spiritual blessings signified by circumcision on account of the Covenant, carried with them external privileges, and identified the chosen nation of Israel. But these external privileges arose from the spiritual blessings which were contained and described in the Covenant.

Calvin draws attention to the fact that there seems to have been a custom, prior to this time, for human covenants to be not only committed to public records, but also to be engraven in brass, or sculptured on stones, in order that the memory of them might be more fully recorded, in the same way that God inscribed His Covenant in the flesh of Abraham and others.

Although the carrying out of this rite of circumcision was commanded by God, as a duty, yet a promise of power from God was added to the command: ''the LORD thy God will circumcise thine heart, and the heart of thy seed, to love the LORD thy God with all thine heart, and with all thy soul, that thou mayest live'' [Deut.30: 6.] — Just in the same way as promises of grace, in the New Testament, are added to commands of duty.

Between the visible outward sign and the spiritual mystery there was a sacramental relationship, and it is in this way that circumcision is called the ''token of the Covenant'' (Gen.17: 11), the ''sign and seal of the Covenant'' (Rom.4: 11), and the ''Covenant'' itself (Gen.17: 9, 10; Acts 7:8)

In this connection the following comment by Calvin on Genesis 17 is interesting: ''Since circumcision is called, by Moses, the Covenant of God, we thence infer that the promise of grace was included in it. For had it been only a mark or token of external profession among men, the name of ''Covenant'' would be by no means suitable; for a Covenant is not otherwise confirmed, than as faith answers to it. And it is common to all sacraments to have the Word of God annexed to them, by which He testifies that He is propitious to us, and calls us to the hope of salvation; yea a sacrament is nothing else than a visible word, or sculpture and image of that grace of God, which the Word more fully illustrates''.

Now let us see what ends circumcision served and for which it was instituted and ordained by God: (1) It was a convictive sign of man's natural corruption, referred to by Jeremiah (by implication) as the circumcision of the heart (Jer.9: 26). (2) It stood for the removal of defilement. It signified and sealed that cleansing which would alone fit the person for the presence of Jehovah, the putting off of this body of sin in the virtue of Christ's death (Col.2: 11). (3) It was "a seal of the righteousness of faith" (Rom.4: 11). (4) It was ordained to be a discriminating mark between God's Covenant people and all others in the world who were strangers to the Covenant (Eph.2:12). Accordingly, the two parties were denominated "the circumcision" and "the uncircumcision", respectively (Col.3: 11; Eph.2: 11) (5) It was also a sign obliging Abraham and his seed to walk with God in the uprightness and sincerity of their hearts, looking to Christ for righteousness; not their own obedience. (6) Finally, as circumcision prefigured Christ who was to come — this holy circumcised *seed* of Abraham (Gal.3: 16), and as His *death* was pointed at in this rite, of necessity this ordinance had to vanish at the death of Christ, and did so. The circumcision of the flesh became the "circumcision of Christ" (Col.2: 11), which expression appertains to the benefits accruing to the Christian due to his union with Christ.

So we see something of the nature and purpose and significance of this sacrament of circumcision; remembering that the sacraments are "to help, promote and confirm faith ... They aid the Word in strengthening faith". There must be alongside the sign, the solid substance of the promise contained in the Word on which faith "may support itself, and from which it may confirm its own assurance. And although we must maintain the distinction between the Word and the sign, yet ... as soon as the sign itself meets our eyes the Word ought to sound in our ears". [Quotes from Calvin's commentary on Gen. ch.17.]

NEW TESTAMENT SACRAMENTS

Only two sacraments are known and administered by the Church in the New Testament era, Baptism and the Lord's Supper. These are both equally signs and seals and intended to be attached to the Word. The word "sacrament" comes from the Latin term SACRAMENTUM and is equivalent to the Greek term MYSTERION which in the New Testament denotes the divine plan of salvation hidden in past ages but now brought to light in the preaching of the Word (Rom.16:25, 26) They are called "mysteries" or "sacraments" because they have enabled men to participate in the mysterious union of God and man through the atoning death and resurrection of Christ. It was Augustine who first gave the general definition of a sacrament, which later became traditional, as ''an outward and temporal sign of an inward and enduring grace''. According to the catechism of the Book of Common Prayer a sacrament is ''an outward and visible sign of an inward and spiritual grace''. The Reformers insisted that the sacraments were given to serve the Word of God. The predominant purpose of a sacrament is for a sign and a seal. It is to declare to *us* what God has done *for* us and *to* us and *within* us. And as we have observed already, God said to Abraham that the seal of the Covenant was not only to be given to *him* but also to his infant off-spring, who were to be circumcised as soon as they were eight days old. So this was a significant development.

From the time of Abraham to the coming of the Messiah in the flesh, the people, including those who had no natural descent from Abraham, but were Gentile proselytes, whom God had called out of the fallen world of mankind, together with their infant seed, made up the Church, and the remaining great mass of Gentiles were ''without Christ, being aliens from the commonwealth of Israel, and strangers from the covenants of promise, (the many publications of the Covenant)having no hope, and without God in the world'' (Eph.2: 12). But at the advent of the Messiah the privileges of the Covenant were no longer limited to the Jews and proselytes and their infant seed, but the door of faith was opened generally and fully to the Gentiles (Acts 14: 27). This was no sudden change of mind on God's part, but rather the fulfilment of something that He had long ago given advance notice of in the pronouncements of His Old Testament prophets. ''In that day there shall be a root of Jesse, (i.e. the Messiah) which shall stand for an ensign of the people; (which shall become an outstandng ensign which all nations may recognise) to it shall the Gentiles seek'' (Is.11: 10). ''Behold, I will lift up mine hand to the Gentiles, (I will call them to Me) and set up my standard to the people: and they shall bring thy sons (sons of the Church) in their arms, and thy daughters shall be carried upon their shoulders'' (Is.49: 22) — and this same truth is seen in many other prophecies.

The opening of the door of faith to the Gentiles coincided with the Jews' rejection of the Messiah and the formal breaking off of the nation of Israel from the Church. At this point we find Paul putting the question: ''Hath God cast away His people?'' then to correct any wrong impression along these lines Paul says: ''God hath not cast away *His people which He foreknew*'' (Rom.11: 1, 2). ''Because of unbelief *they* were broken off, and *thou* standest by faith'' (Rom.11: 20). It is clear from this, and the teaching of the whole of chapter 11, that at this point we have arrived at a very critical and sensitive stage in the whole economy of God.

As we have noticed earlier, there is but *one* Covenant of Grace and *one* Church. *Before* the advent of the Messiah, the believing people of God, and their infant seed, were parties to the Covenant, and the mark of circumcision was given to them as a sign of their inclusion in the Covenant and in the Church. As we have seen also, this was true not only of Jews but also of Gentile proselytes. When the *unbelieving* Jews were formally broken off from the Church, both parents and children together, the *believing* Gentiles were implanted, or engrafted, in their place. On account of this change, it is reasonable to say that these believing Gentiles, which were as truly Abraham's seed as the believing Jews were, [''If ye be Christ's''; (this is the distinguishing criterion) ''then are ye Abraham's seed, and heirs according to the promise'' (Gal.3: 29)], and being engrafted into the Church, were in the same position and so enjoyed all the same privileges of the Covenant for themselves, and for their infant seed, as the believing Jews had done. It would be unreasonable to think that the benefits of the Covenant were changed at this juncture, having in mind that they constitute blessings and privileges determined by God. If the infant seed were included in the Jewish era, as undoubtedly they were (''Every man child among you shall be circumcised . . . and it shall be a token of the Covenant'') (Gen.17: 10, 11), then God must have intended it to be included in the Christian era also. As soon as the Church entered the Christian era, and the believing Gentiles were by faith added to it, the children of those believing Gentiles are declared to be federally holy (1 Cor.7: 14). The reference to being unclean or holy is, as we know, not to their *spiritual* standing but their *federal* standing; in other words, it means that the children of believing parents, due solely to their being *their* children (even if only one of the two parents is a believer) are constituted holy in this federal sense, or rather, they are reckoned within the Covenant, and so in the Church.

The godly Zacharias, father of John the Baptist, being filled with the Holy Ghost, and so enabled to prophesy, spoke of the continuing validity of the Covenant of Grace, saying: "Blessed be the Lord God of Israel; for He hath visited and redeemed His people, and hath raised up an horn of salvation for us in the house of His servant David; as He spake by the mouth of His holy prophets, which have been since the world began: that we should be saved from our enemies, and from the hand of all that hate us; to perform the mercy promised to our fathers, and to remember His holy Covenant; the oath which He sware to our father Abraham" (Luke l: 68–73). Quite evidently the Covenant confirmed to Abraham was a Gospel Covenant.

Quite understandably, at this point of transition from the Jewish era to the Christian, there was provided by God a *new* seal of the Covenant. Circumcision, having been embodied in the ceremonial law by Moses, was the sign used by the Jews until the sacrifice of the Messiah, who "abolished in His flesh . . . the law of commandments" (Eph.2:15) (the ceremonial law). Even Jesus Himself was circumcised, when He was eight days old (Luk.2:21). Which event provides evidence of the truth of His statement that He came not to destroy the Law but to fulfil it (Matt.5: 17 & 3: 15). But after the sacrifice at Calvary the rite of circumcision was abolished, and it was the risen Lord Himself who instituted its substituted rite of baptism, in His great commission — "Go ye therefore, and teach all nations (or make disciples of all nations), baptising them in the name of the Father, and of the Son, and of the Holy Ghost" (Matt.28: 19).

That the token and seal of baptism serves the same end that circumcision formerly did, is evident from the apostle Paul's words in his epistle to the Gentiles at Colosse. Having told them that they were complete in Christ, he goes on to say "In whom also ye *are* circumcised" — (Col.2: 11). Paul is here implying that they must not listen to those false teachers who were suggesting that they need to be physically circumcised in order to be true followers of, and believers in, Christ; and then he goes on to tell them that they had already received a far superior sort of circumcision "Ye *are* circumcised with the circumcision made *without* hands, in putting off the body of the sins of the flesh (fallen nature) by the circumcision of Christ: buried with Him in baptism, wherein also ye are risen —" (Col.2: 12)

SIGNIFICANCE OF BAPTISM

This seems to be the right place to consider briefly the significance, and efficacy, and meaning, of baptism as the newly introduced token of the Covenant. And although it is a *new* token, replacing the *former* token of circumcision, it is evident that the significance of the Covenant's sign and seal, whether circumcision or baptism, is uniform throughout the ages. So we must be careful not to assign a significance and meaning to the new rite which could not be applied before. The chief emphasis must be placed on union with Christ; this is what it is chiefly pointing at and representing. The very nature of the rite, and the predominant role the water plays in the outward visible sign, tends to put the emphasis on the idea of cleansing, but although this is very definitely involved, and is important, it does not occupy the *chief* position. "Baptising them in the name . . ." (meaning "into" the name) — Matt.28:19. It is this notion of baptising *into* that is significant. We find the same expression in 1 Cor. 10:2 — ". . . baptised into Moses" and 1 Cor.1: 13 "baptised into the name of Paul". This expresses a relationship to the person into whom, or whose name, people are baptised. The kind of relationship with which we are concerned here is clear from various Scriptures. Perhaps one will suffice. "As many of you as have been baptised into Christ have put on Christ. . . . ye are all one in Christ Jesus" (Gal.3: 27, 28). A clear reference to union with Christ; union with Him in His death, burial and resurrection; even including our position in Him in heavenly places (Eph.1: 3 & 2:6). The Westminster Confession of Faith describes baptism, amongst other things, as a sign and seal of the Covenant of Grace and of a person's engrafting into Christ. The Baptist Confession of Faith of 1689 also describes it, amongst other things, as a sign of a person "being engrafted into Christ". It is not *only* union with *Christ,* but also with the Father and with the Holy Spirit.

However, having stressed the importance of this aspect of union, it is important that we also bear in mind the notion of purification, which also is contained in the rite. There are two aspects in which purification is represented in the rite, and which takes place in the person, at the inception of the relationship with Christ; they are purification from the *defilement* and purification from the *guilt* of sin. Purification from the *defilement* of sin is equivalent to regeneration. Having in mind that baptism is the circumcision of the New Testament, and that circumcision symbolised purification from defilement, we may even *from this* infer that this is also symbolised in baptism. Purification from the *guilt* of sin, equivalent to justification, is seen to be represented in baptism in Acts 2: 38: ''be baptised . . . for the remission (pardon) of sins''. Also Acts 22: 16. ''arise, and be baptised, and wash away thy *sins*''. And again, referring to baptism Peter says ''not the putting away of the filth of the flesh, (that is the outward sign) but the answer (mirrored in the outward sign) of a good conscience toward God'' (1 Peter 3: 21). In other words, purification from the *guilt* of sin by the sprinkling of the blood of Christ.

In addition to the foregoing, we must bear in mind that baptism is a means of grace, but not a means of conferring the grace represented. It is a means of grace to signify and confirm grace, but not to impart grace.

This is what John Murray has to say about the efficacy of baptism:— ''The efficacy of baptism, in all cases, is that it is God's testimony to, and seal upon, the reality and security of the grace which He bestows in accordance with the provisions of the Covenant of Grace. And this grace is nothing less than union with the three persons of the Godhead, in the unity expressed by their joint possession of the one name, and in the richness of the distinctive relationship which each person of the Godhead sustains to the people of God in the economy of the Covenant of Grace.''

The unbelieving Jews were superstitiously fond of circumcision and it was because of this that Paul wrote what he did to the Colossians. It was also because of the need to emphasise the truth being signified, rather than the sign itself, that he wrote the following to the Church at Rome: ''For he is not a Jew, which is one outwardly; neither is that circumcision, which is outward in the flesh: but he is a Jew, which is one inwardly; and circumcision is that of the heart, in the spirit, and not in the letter; whose praise is not of men, but of God'' (Rom.2: 28, 29). And for the same reason Paul wrote to the Galatians: ''For in Jesus Christ neither circumcision availeth any thing, nor uncircumcision; but faith which worketh by love'' — (Gal.5: 6.) — ''For in Christ Jesus neither circumcision availeth any thing, nor uncircumcision, but a new creature'' (Gal.6: 15).

It was because of the Jews' emphasis on the continuing need for circumcision that the apostle Peter also is found exhorting and persuading the unbelieving and convicted Jews to believe, and submit themselves to baptism, in Acts 2: 38, 39. Peter reminds them of the terms of the still operative Covenant ''the promise is unto you, and to your children''. There seems to be an implication here that Peter is saying: ''You and your children bear the marks of the Covenant in your bodies, which cannot be expunged, and which have been assuring you that you and your infants are participants in the Covenant. Do not imagine that because I am telling you that the token of circumcision, as such, in you and your children, is no longer valid, and that you must repent and believe in Christ's atoning death *alone* for your participation in the Covenant, that your children are now not recognised; you being *in* the Covenant and they *outside*? ''No,'' says Peter, ''here is the new sign of the Covenant — baptism — and it is for your children also, because the promise is for *them*, as well as for you. Remember what the promise is: 'I will establish My Covenant between Me and thee and thy seed after thee in their generations for an *everlasting* Covenant, to be a God unto thee, and to thy seed after thee' '' (Gen.17: 7). In this way Peter showed them how that ancient promise was *still valid* and would be then as effectually sealed to them and their children *by baptism* as it was in the former era *by circumcision*. Also that the Gentiles, which were then yet ''afar off'', whenever God should call them, would equally enjoy the same privileges, both for themselves and for their children.

I have in this section considered the signs and seals of the Covenant of Grace, and how the seal under the Jewish era was that of circumcision, and the seal under the Christian era is that of baptism. I have brought to view the fact that the seal and the privileges of the Covenant under the *Jewish era* were enjoyed by believing parents *and* their seed, resulting from a divine command, and have drawn the parallel between that and the *Christian era*, showing how that the privileges of believing parents under the latter era, being one of expanded horizons, rather than contracted ones, should not be anything less than those of the former. Bishop J. C. Ryle wrote: "The general tendency of the Gospel is to increase men's spiritual privileges and not to diminish them." It is upon these grounds that the case for infant baptism stands. I realise that questions will still remain in people's minds on certain points, especially regarding the spiritual standing of infants who have been baptised, but these things I propose to deal with in the next section, together with other matters which have been the grounds of disagreement amongst God's people regarding this rite of baptism.

★ ★ ★

"I will pour My Spirit upon thy seed, and My blessing upon thine offspring: and they shall spring up as among the grass, as willows by the water courses."

Isaiah 44:3, 4.

"Suffer the little children to come unto Me, and forbid them not: for of such is the kingdom of God. — And He took them up in His arms, put His hands upon them, and blessed them."

Mark 10:14, 16.

INFANT BAPTISM

In this and the following section — "The Mode of Baptism" — I have drawn very freely from the contents of a book written by John Murray entitled "Christian Baptism". As there would appear to be little doubt that the question as to whether there is Scriptural warrant for administering baptism to infants, or not, is a matter concerning which God's people have held opposite views over the centuries, we would seem to be justified in looking at this particular aspect of our subject somewhat fully.

It is I think a matter of interest, in passing, although not contributing any Scriptural evidence, albeit providing some corroborative evidence, that those who have maintained the existence of adequate Scriptural warrant for infant baptism, include Reformers of past centuries, both on the Continent and in this Country, such as Cranmer, Ridley, Latimer, Luther, Calvin and Knox; Puritans such as Baxter, Flavel, Watson, Goodwin, Cotton, and Owen; to which company of men we can also add the name of Jonathan Edwards; also Wesley, Whitfield and Chalmers. Their view is also upheld by the declared belief of the Church of Scotland, the Church of England and the Church of Ireland, together with those of the Methodist, Presbyterian and Independent denominations.

The following words are extracted from chapter 28 of The Confession of Faith approved by the General Assembly of the Church of Scotland in 1647 and commonly referred to as the "Westminister Confession of Faith":

> "Baptism is a sacrament of the New Testament, ordained

> by Jesus Christ, to be unto the party baptised a sign and seal of the Covenant of Grace, of his engrafting into Christ, of regeneration, of remission of sins, and of his giving up unto God through Jesus Christ, to walk in newness life: which sacrament is, by Christ's own appointment, to be continued in His Church until the end of the world.
>
> "Dipping of the person into the water is not necessary; but baptism is rightly administered by pouring or sprinkling water upon the person.
>
> "Not only those that do actually profess faith in and obedience unto Christ, but also the infants of one or both believing parents are to be baptised."

The following is an extract from Article 34 of the Belgic Confession. As this is not quite so familiar to us in this Country, nor its origin so well known, the following details extracted from it, provide us, I believe, some ground for confidence in its articles of faith. The chief author of the Confession "was Guido de Brès, a preacher of the Reformed Churches of the Netherlands, who died a martyr to the faith in the year 1567. During the sixteenth century the churches in this Country were exposed to the most terrible persecution by the Roman Catholic government. To protest against this cruel oppression, and to prove to the persecutors that the adherents of the Reformed faith were no rebels, as was laid to their charge, but law-abiding citizens who professed the true Christian doctrine according to the Holy Scriptures, de Brès prepared this Confession in the year 1561. In the following year a copy was sent to King Philip II, together with an address in which the petitioners declared that they were ready to obey the government in "all lawful things, but that they would 'offer their backs to stripes, their tongues to knives, their mouths to gags, and their whole bodies to the fire,' rather than deny the truth expressed in this Confession."

Having just referred to "the error of the Anabaptists", Article 34 of the Confession goes on — "who are not content with the one only baptism they have once received, and moreover condemn the baptism of the infants of believers, who we believe ought to be baptised and sealed with the sign of the Covenant, as the children of Israel formerly were circumcised upon the same promises which are made unto our children. And indeed Christ shed His blood no less for the washing of the children of believers than for adult persons; and therefore they ought to receive the sign and sacrament of that which Christ has done for them; . . . Moreover what circumcision was to the Jews, baptism is to our children. And for this reason Paul calls baptism the 'circumcision of Christ' ".

The following is an extract from the Heidelberg Catechism. As in the case of the Belgic Confession, and for the same reason, I give the following details extracted from this Catechism. "It is called the Heidelberg Catechism because it originated in Heidelberg, the capital of the German Electorate of the Palatinate, at the behest of the Elector, Frederick III. In order that the Calvinistic Reformation might gain the ascendancy in his domain, this pious ruler charged Zacharias Ursinus, professor at the Heidelberg University, and Caspar Olevianus, the court preacher, with the preparation of a manual for catechetical instruction. The result was a new Catechism, which, after having been approved by the Elector himself and by a gathering of prominent Calvinists, was published in the beginning of the year 1563 . . . At the present day (1972) the Heidelberg Catechism still has the distinction of being the most influential and the most generally accepted of the several Catechisms of Reformation times." Question 74 of this Catechism asks: "Are infants also to be baptised?" Answer: "Yes; for since they, as well as adults, are included in the Covenant and Church of God, and since both redemption from sin, and the Holy Spirit the Author of faith, are through the blood of Christ promised to them no less than to adults ("I will pour My Spirit upon thy seed, and My blessing upon thine offspring" Is.44: 3), they must also by baptism, as a sign of the Covenant, be distinguished from the children of unbelievers, as was done in the old Covenant or testament by circumcision instead of which baptism was instituted in the new Covenant."

Before moving on to any further positive statements in support of the administration of baptism to infants, it might perhaps clear the ground somewhat to consider what baptism does *not* imply.

Bishop Ryle of Liverpool wrote: "I wish to urge on many of my fellow Churchmen the dangerous tendency to extravagantly high views of the efficacy of baptism. I have no wish to conceal my meaning. I refer to those Churchmen who maintain that grace invariably accompanies baptism, and that all baptised infants are in baptism born again. . . . They seem to me, and to many others, to degrade a holy ordinance appointed by Christ into a mere charm, which is to act mechanically like a medicine acting on the body, without any movement of a man's heart or soul. Surely this is dangerous!''

It is important, and gratifying, that this statement has been made, because there is no doubt whatsoever that many Churchmen, either wittingly or unwittingly, give the impression that they believe that when an infant is baptised it is automatically regenerated. This is evident from the following extract from ''The Book of Common Prayer'': — ''Seeing now, dearly beloved brethren, that this child is by baptism regenerate . . .'' Then again from the catechism in the same ''Book'': — ''Question: What is required of persons to be baptised? Answer: Repentance, whereby they forsake sin; and faith, whereby they steadfastly believe the promises of God . . . .'' Question: Why then are infants baptised, when by reason of their tender age they cannot perform them'' (i.e. repentance and faith); Answer: Because they promise them both by their sureties; which promise, when they come to age, themselves are bound to perform.''

A well respected Churchman, Henry Budd, in his book ''Infant Baptism. The Means of National Reformation'' expounds this view of infant baptism. He writes: ''A brother is assumed elect at baptism and the Church's dealings with him through to burial is with the same assumption that he is elect.'' And again — ''It is as the elect of God . . . that the child is introduced into the Church at baptism . . . the Church praying that he may ever *remain* in the number of His faithful and elect children.''

It appears to me that even some eminent and godly Churchmen have confused themselves, and others also, by introducing the subject of election into the discussion at this point. They refer to ''presumptive election'' or ''presumptive regeneration'', but these terms, whatever they may have been intended to mean, are far too suggestive to avoid ambiguity and confusion. Let it be stated as clearly as possible that the sign or seal of circumcision or baptism, for an infant or an adult, does not bring into existence that which is signified or sealed. The recipient of baptism is *not* introduced into the Church at baptism as the elect of God. The elect of God they may or may not be, but this is not determined by baptism, nor is it the responsibility, nor within the capability of man to determine it.

One principle, which is embedded in the foundations of the Christian faith, and which must therefore always be taken into consideration whenever seeking to arrive at an understanding of any tenet of the truth, is this. Mankind is individually responsible and answerable to God. Every individual, adult and infant alike, is born in sin and is a child of wrath. On account of this, no person can enter into the Kingdom of God (or the Church) without being born again. Peter tells us that an individual is born again "by the Word of God" (l Peter 1: 23) that is to say by apprehending the message of the Scriptures, and this is only possible when God opens the eyes of the understanding and so enables a person to apprehend God's offer of mercy and forgiveness held forth in the Gospel in the person of the Lord Jesus Christ and Him crucified; and to trust in Him and believe and embrace the promise. This is the bedrock of the Christian faith. There is no Scriptural warrant for a person to exercise faith *on behalf of another,* however young that other may be. Every infant is under an inescapable duty to make an intelligent response to the Gospel, as soon as God gives him (or her) the ability to do so. Only God knows when that point has been reached; and the destiny, of an infant who dies before that point *is* reached, is in the hands of God and subject to His secret disposal, and we must leave it there, surrounded with a cloud of prevenient prayers.

God has, however, graciously provided a ray of hope, emanating from His Word, for a parent sorrowing over the loss of a little child. King David sorrowed over the sickness of his child. Then the child died, and David said, "Can I bring him back again? I shall go to him, but he shall not return to me" (2 Sam.12: 23). The initial meaning being that both David and his child were going to the same place — the grave. But the expression holds out sufficient hope to keep us from despairing, but not sufficient to make us presumptuous, that there will be a meeting in heaven, in such a case.

More could be said. There seems to be very little doubt that misguided endeavours, such as those described above, concerning the right of infants of believing parents to receive baptism, have marred the case for infant baptism based on Scriptural evidence. I will now proceed with some positive evidence.

POSITIVE EVIDENCE

It is important that we retain in our minds clear views of the significance of baptism. William Cunningham (1805–1861) in his ''Historical Theology'' makes the following excellent statement in this connection. He has just been making a number of observations on the general allegation that infant baptism is inconsistent with some of the qualities or properties of the ordinance of baptism. Then he goes on to say that the leading allegation of the anti-paedobaptists on this particular aspect of the subject is, ''that it is inconsistent with the nature of baptism, as set before us in Scripture, that it should be administered to any, except upon the ground of a previous possession of saving faith by the person receiving it. If this proposition could be established, it would, of course, preclude the baptism of infants who have not such faith, and who could not profess it if they had it. We are persuaded that this proposition cannot be established, though we admit that a good deal which is plausible can be adduced from Scripture in support of it. ... But in the absence of anything which, directly or by implication, teaches that the previous profession of faith is of *the essence* of the ordinance, and universally necessary to its legitimate administration and reception, an inference of this sort is not sufficient to neutralise the direct and positive evidence we have in Scripture in favour of the baptism of infants.''

I have included the foregoing quotation so as to provide a background to Cunningham's further important statement which seems to be particularly relevant at this point. The statement reads as follows: ''The only thing which seems to be really of the essence of the ordinance (i.e. baptism) in this respect is, that the parties receiving it are capable of possessing, and have a federal interest in, the promise of the spiritual blessings which it was intended to signify and to seal. Now the blessings which baptism was intended to signify and seal are justification and regeneration, —

that is, the washing away of guilt, and the washing away of depravity. . . . *Faith* does not stand in the same relation to baptism as these blessings do, and for this obvious and conclusive reason, that it *is not directly and expressly signified or represented in the external ordinance itself, as they are.*'' [Author's italics].

Perhaps the following review may help to consolidate and summarise the understanding of the significance of baptism as deduced from the Scriptures and as represented in this treatise.

There is only one Covenant of Grace, valid from the beginning to the end of time, containing all the promises of God's grace to sinful mankind, and made over to every individual believer in Christ. God gave to Abraham the associated sign and seal of the Covenant — circumcision (Gen.17: 1–14). God also gave a *command* to Abraham that every man child *in his household* should receive this sign. He did not say: ''He that has the same saving faith as you have'' but He said ''he that is born in the house''. It is in terms of this Covenant that Abraham is the father of all the faithful (Rom.4: 11), not only in the Jewish economy, but also in the Christian economy. It is in terms of this Covenant that the blessing of Abraham comes upon the Gentiles as the Covenant is unfolded in the New Testament.

We know that the sign of circumcision did not bring Abraham into the Covenant; it confirmed that he was *in* it. It was ''a seal of the *righteousness* [Author's italics] of the faith which he had yet being uncircumcised'' (Rom.4: 11).

We know also that Abraham's circumcised infant child did not receive faith through the sign of circumcision. He was not regenerated by that rite. Indeed, *nothing* happened to him spiritually. The significance of circumcision for the child was this. He received circumcision because it was God's command, and this was a sign that even as God had received Abraham into the Church according to the Covenant, so He recognised Abraham's family as part of Abraham himself. His children were *federally holy* and separate from the rest of the world. It signified this external privilege as well as the deeper spiritual privileges of God's grace. It put the child *in the way of blessing*.

Thomas Shepard, discussing this point, and having referred to the apostle Paul's words in 1 Cor.7: 14, where Paul says that the children of believing parents are federally holy, Shepard goes on to say "and if federally holy, then of the Church (for real holiness cannot here be meant), and in the Covenant of it; even as it is said (Deut.7: 6) "thou art an holy people unto the LORD thy God", few of which number were really and savingly holy; but they were all so *federally*, or by Covenant, and so became God's special Church or people."

It is very pertinent, in the light of the foregoing, to enquire what is the status of the infants of believing parents if they are *not* within the Covenant and so, federally holy? If they *are* in the Covenant then they must receive its sign and seal, otherwise they will be in a sort of spiritual no-man's-land.

There then is the plain evidence of Scripture of the origin of the divine ordinance by which God appended signs and seals to His Covenant of Grace. We are not called upon to enquire why God did this, all we know is that He did it, and "He hath done all things well". Some might ask whether the situation would not have been the same without the sign of circumcision. The Covenant would certainly have been the same, but it seems to me that this is an area of speculation into which we must not enter. Circumcision was the command of God, and it confirmed the Covenant to Abraham and his whole family; his wife and children, *including Ishmael.*

How can we explain the circumcision of Ishmael? Clearly we cannot explain it by saying that Abraham made a mistake. It was prior to the circumcision of Ishmael (Gen.17: 23) that God said to Abraham "My Covenant will I establish (or rather — "carry out") with Isaac." There are obligations and promises in the Covenant, and this particular aspect is being brought out in this section of the treatise. Here is Abraham carrying out the explicit command of God in circumcising Ishmael. But subsequent events reveal the fact that Ishmael was *not* one of God's chosen people. Is this a difficulty? No there is no difficulty, but rather this situation helpfully highlights the fact that when God commanded Abraham to circumcise *all* his male infants, and that all believing parents should do likewise, He meant just exactly what He said, regardless of whether or not the infant, having received the seal of the Covenant, on growing up proved to be a believer. For Abraham to have refused to circumcise Ishmael would have been a direct violation of the divine command. That was one *most important* aspect of this rite — the command of God. The *other* aspect being the fact that the seal of the Covenant did not indicate that its recipient had received the spiritual blessings which it represented, as was evident in the case of Ishmael, who did *not* receive them. This was according to the determinate counsel of God.

Although circumcision and baptism are the signs and seals of Covenant union and communion with Christ, carrying the deepest possible *spiritual* significance, as well as signifying *external* privileges, it does not follow that every individual who bears this sign and seal is an actual *partaker* of the grace signified and sealed. It frequently happens that due to inadequate examination of candidates for baptism, individuals receive the sign of baptism when they are not qualified to receive it. But in addition to this, even when all the divinely instituted safeguards have been applied (and beyond this, church officers are not called upon to go) it does not follow of necessity that the rite of baptism guarantees that the recipient is in possession of the grace signified. These are matters of fact which must be accepted and cannot be denied. However, this situation must not be allowed to diminish, to the slightest extent, the fullest significance of the rite. We must recognise the existence of a discrepancy between the secret operations and purposes of God in His saving grace, *on the one hand*, and the divinely instituted method of administering the Covenant in the world (employing fallible sinful men in its administration) *on the other*.

Relevant to this situation the following remarks, made by the godly Archbishop Usher in 1624, are of interest: "Some have the outward sign, and not the inward grace. Some have the inward grace, and not the outward sign. We must not commit idolatry by deifying the outward element."

We looked in the previous section at Scriptural evidence to show how the crucifixion of the Messiah was the transition point between circumcision and baptism. This was a critical and sensitive point in the history of the Church. At this time there were many Jewish families whose participation in the Covenant was signified by the mark of circumcision. Their children were one with them. Notwithstanding the fact that, due to spiritual apathy, many of these families were without saving faith — but they thought that Abraham was their spiritual father.

This was the situation confronting Peter on the Day of Pentecost, when in response to the people's urgent enquiry "What shall we do?" he said "Repent and be baptised every one of you . . . for the promise is unto you, and to your children —". Implying — "do not imagine that your children will be excluded now (Acts 2: 38, 39). The promise of the Covenant still stands as we have it in Gen.17 and particularly verse 7".

So at this point we have a comprehensive view of New Testament teaching on baptism. In just the same way as the *adult* Abraham received the sign of circumcision, as representing the righteousness which he had by the faith which God had given him to believe His promises — "a seal of the righteousness of the faith which he had "(Rom.4: 11) so, Abraham's male *infants* also received the mark of the Covenant, simply because they were Abraham's children.

In exactly the same way, the *adult* Jews listening to Peter, were called to repent and believe on the Lord Jesus Christ for remission of sins; and if they *did* believe, then the righteousness associated with this faith was to be confirmed by receiving baptism, as the seal of the Covenant, as earlier instituted by the Lord Himself. Peter implied that if they were eligible to receive the newly appointed seal of the Covenant, *so were their children,* according to the ancient promise and command of God to Abraham.

It is evident from the Scriptures that there were many Jews who had been circumcised, but who did not have true faith. "But", asks Paul, "shall their unbelief make the faith of God without effect? God forbid" (Rom.3: 3). So some Jews (natural branches) were broken off from the olive tree (the Church) because of *unbelief* (Rom.11: 20). However "God is able to graff them in again" (v.23) *by faith*. For this reason Peter called upon these Jews on the Day of Pentecost to repent and believe, that they might be "graffed in".

D. M. Lloyd-Jones commenting on this 11th chapter of Paul's epistle to the Romans says, "The olive tree is a picture of the true Church. There were first natural branches in it — that is, the Jews. But some of these have been plucked out because of their unbelief; and now unnatural branches, the Gentiles, are grafted in. But it is the same tree, it is the same trunk. . . . Because God is one, there is only one way of salvation, whether under the Old Testament or the New. . . . There is only one way of being reconciled to God. It is the same Covenant of Grace then, now, and in the future.''

Here then are the grounds for adult baptism, in the case of the adults previously being unbelievers and never having been baptised before. Such people being required, before being accepted for baptism, to give an intelligent and credible profession of their faith. Following the analogy of Scripture the children of such newly converted adult believers (even if only one parent has so far been converted) must be given the sign of the Covenant — baptism — otherwise they would be federally unclean (1 Cor.7: 14) and out of the way of blessing. The proper ground of baptism, both for infants and adults, consists in the divine institution and command; which regulates the Church in all elements of her worship and her sacraments.

The inward cause that moved God to take the Jews and their children into the Church and Covenant in the Old Testament era was the same as moves Him in the Christian era. This can be said because the only cause why the Lord did this for the Jews and their children was His love and free grace and mercy. ''Because He loved thy fathers, therefore He chose their seed ''(Deut.4: 37). Shepard commenting on this verse says —'' which choosing is not by eternal election, or choosing to glory, for many of their seed never came to glory, but unto this privilege, to be His people above all others in outward Covenant with Him . . . And hence (Deut.10: 15) because 'the Lord had a delight in thy fathers to love them', hence He chose their seed''. From whence Shepard argues that ''the same love respects the seed of His people *now,* as *then* it did. And therefore, if *then* because He loved *them* He chose *their* seed to be of His Church, so in *these* days, because He loveth *us,* he chooseth *our* seed to be of His church also.''

In Deut.29: 10–13 Moses has solemnly gathered together the whole company before God, mentioning the various categories by name including ''your little ones'', and declares the purpose of the occasion — ''that thou shouldest enter into Covenant with the LORD thy God, and into His oath, which the LORD thy God maketh with thee this day: that He may establish thee to-day for a people unto Himself, and that He may be unto thee a God, as He hath said unto thee, and as He hath sworn unto thy fathers, to

Abraham, to Isaac, and to Jacob.''

By the very nature of things it would be impossible for the infant male Jew to be re-circumcised when he came of age. This teaching us that neither is it required that an infant, who has been baptised, be re-baptised when coming of age. The Anabaptists did not recognise infant baptism to be valid baptism, and so they baptised *again* those who had received baptism as infants, and hence came into being their name, which means ''twice baptised''. But if we bear in mind the significance of baptism, and the fact that it does not stand as a mark of spiritual attainment, but rather as representing symbolically the deep spiritual realities of salvation, the mark of circumcision, or baptism, speaks just as loudly of those realities in the infant as it does in the adult. Baptism *represents* something that is performed in an individual *once only* and is never repeated. A person can only be united to Christ *once*; and once united that person is united for ever.

It might be questioned what was the position with regard to the females in the time of Abraham. Again we must rest on the command of God. A sign confirming the Covenant was to be made in the flesh of the males only. We know that God's promises were made, and were applicable, to male and female alike. Females had need of the confirmation as well as the males, and God knew this. We can rest assured ''that the symbol was ordained for the sake of both sexes'' [Calvin on Genesis], not only the believing father and his infant sons, but also his wife and infant daughters.

I have referred so far to the Scriptural warrant for baptising the infants of believing parents, and to the fact that there was a divine command for believing parents to administer to their male infants the Jewish equivalent to baptism, as a sign of the everlasting Covenant. Although this Scriptural warrant provides sufficient grounds for the administering of baptism to infants, having in mind the widespread disagreement amongst God's people concerning this matter (notwithstanding their highest esteem of the unique and final authority of Scripture), it may help to dispel the reservations of some, if consideration be given to certain corroborating evidence.

CORROBORATING EVIDENCE

I will therefore now refer to some such evidence. The baptism of children is nowhere forbidden in the New Testament. And we must bear in mind, as already observed, that many of the first Christians were Jews who had been accustomed to having their children admitted into the Covenant by the solemn ordinance of circumcision, as a matter of course. Without a distinct prohibition from the Lord Jesus Christ the Jews would naturally go on with the same procedure and bring their children to receive the new sign of the Covenant — baptism. The absence of any divine command to the contrary leads us to assume that infants in the Christian era are to receive the sign of the Covenant in the same way as God commanded them to do in the Jewish era.

There are, furthermore, instances of household baptism, recorded in the New Testament, which would inevitably involve the baptism of any infants where included in such a household. There is no specific proof of infants *being* included, but the significant point is that household baptism was practised. Whilst only twelve instances of baptism are recorded in the New Testament at least three of these refer to household baptism.

It is recorded in the Gospel narratives how the Lord Jesus Christ displayed more than a passing interest in little children: "Suffer little children, and forbid them not, to come unto Me" (Matt.19: 14). And then: "... these little ones which believe in Me" (Matt.18: 6). Certainly it can be said that the children referred to in Matt.18 were old enough to understand the Gospel and believe in the Saviour. However, we read of children being *brought* to Him (Mark 10: 13). This narrative suggests that these children were infants in arms, and it is important to notice that they were capable of receiving some benefit from the Lord even though they were too young to understand what was happening. "He took them up in His arms, put His hands upon them and blessed them" (Mark 10: 16). But another record leaves us in *no doubt* regarding the infancy of those brought to Him. "And they brought unto Him also infants, that He would touch them ..." (Luke 18: 15). The Greek word translated "infants" is BREPHOS meaning infants or babes. Jesus said "suffer little children to come unto Me" — v.16. From these passages of Scripture we recognise our Lord's awareness of the fact that even babes were capable of receiving divine blessing.

LOCAL IMPLICATIONS OF INFANT BAPTISM

We will next consider the implications and responsibilities, and also the discipline, associated with the administration of infant baptism in a local church, which is large enough (for the sake of the illustration) to include several families. Let us suppose that there is an unbelieving young man who has for a little while been attending the services, and by the grace of God has been converted, and becomes a Christian. This young man, having requested baptism, is then examined by officers of the church, and as he was able to give a satisfactory confession of faith in Jesus Christ, the sign and seal of baptism was in due course administered to him. Subsequently he fell in love with a Christian young woman who had been baptised as an infant. They were married and eventually had a baby boy. The father and mother have the seal of the Covenant relation in their baptism. They then request that their baby boy be baptised, which baptism is duly administered, giving to him the seal of the Covenant, thus bringing the whole family into the Covenant relation.

But supposing certain Christian families in the same church had children who had been baptised as infants. Then they grow up in the church. Because they have been baptised as infants they have received the mark of the Covenant. What is their standing as they grow up? Is it assumed that they are Christian? No personal confession of faith had of course preceded their baptism.

It should be understood that the mere fact of being baptised in infancy does not entitle such people to any of the privileges of the church if, when they come to years of discretion and understanding they show no interest in Covenant responsibilities and privileges. If they are indifferent, and walk contrary to the Gospel, they are to be disciplined accordingly. Confederate members of the church are under the supervision and discipline of the church. If the church is vigilant and faithful, confederate members will be constantly under the instruction of the church, and ordinarily, long before they have children of their own, will be confronted with their Covenant responsibilities and privileges. They will be advised that the Covenant relation, sealed by their baptism in infancy, implies the necessity of their open avowal of that Covenant and their public confession of Christ as their only Saviour and Lord.

In this connection, let us consider the situation where two people, who were baptised as infants, get married and have a child and request baptism for their child. (We are not considering a case of parents who had *not* been baptised requesting baptism for their child, as this would be manifestly irregular). As in the case mentioned earlier, the parents had obviously made no personal confession before their baptism in infancy. If, as mentioned above, they show no interest in Covenant responsibilities, and walk contrary to the Gospel, they are to be disciplined, and one of the ways in which such discipline should be exercised is by denying them the privilege of baptism for their children, until their lives show evidence of the new birth.

But what is the position with regard to parents who were baptised as infants and who *give* evidence in their lives of the new birth? May they receive baptism for their children simply on the basis of their having received the sign of the Covenant themselves when infants, and enjoy confederate membership of the church? It should be pointed out to such parents that their Covenant relation necessitates an open avowal of that Covenant and a public confession of Christ as their only Saviour and Lord. Any who are not prepared to meet this requirement would be liable to discipline, and by the very nature of the rite with respect to infants as outlined above, would not be fit to receive baptism for their children.

As in the case of Abraham, so in the case of believing parents, the sign and seal of the Covenant represent the righteousness received by faith. In other words these things apply to those ''who also walk in the steps of that faith of our father Abraham'' (Rom.4: 12). The degree of faith and assurance that God's promise to such parents will be fulfilled, is proportionate to the extent to which the fear of God, the keeping of His Covenant, and the doing of His commandments, rule in their hearts and lives. Such faithfulness to God's Covenant includes all that is involved in the bringing up of children in the nurture and admonition of the Lord, bearing in mind that the parents are but the delegated instruments of the

Lord in this process of admonition. The more *limited* solidarity which exists in the family, is embraced within a *broader* solidarity which God has established in the church. These two institutions, the family and the church, mutually minister to each other.

SOME OBJECTIONS TO INFANT BAPTISM

Having looked at the direct Scriptural warrant for baptising the infants of believing parents, and also at other considerations by way of corroboration, we will now consider *a few objections* to the practice of infant baptism. Bearing in mind that an unbiased and unprejudiced approach to such a subject as the one before us, demands that fair consideration be given to any arguments contrary to the interpretation outlined in this treatise.

Some of the points which will now be mentioned may already have been touched on, but there is some advantage in gathering these objections under one heading, so that when considered together, and if of substance, they may have the maximum weight and persuasiveness.

(1) The objection which most readily springs to mind is that which is based on the fact that there is no specific command in the Scriptures to baptise infants, nor is there any record of a particular case of an infant receiving the rite of baptism. We must look at this, because for some people this is one of the most persuasive objections, and seems to settle the argument. But the point to be considered is whether it *does* settle the argument, or *not*.

The two facts referred to are undenied, but neither must it be denied that what by good and necessary inference can be *deduced from* Scripture, is of authority, as well as what is expressly set down in Scripture. The arguments contained in this treatise in support of administering baptism to infants fall into the category of ''good and necessary inference'' deduced from Scripture. It could also be added, in this connection, that there are very few instances, recorded in Scripture, of baptism actually being administered to *anyone*.

(2) Another objection very often made to infant baptism is this. It is borne in mind that the essential prerequisite to baptism being administered to an adult person is that the person requesting

baptism must first give a credible and intelligent profession of faith. It is then objected that an infant is incapable of giving such a profession and therefore is not qualified to receive the sign and the seal. However it must be recognised that on such occasions as, for instance, Peter's sermon on the Day of Pentecost and Paul's address to the Philippian jailor, whilst there was a call to repentance and faith, requiring a credible confession, it cannot be proved that as families were baptised there were not included infants, who by the very nature of things would not be capable of giving a credible profession. But this apart, the case for infant baptism does not rest upon supposition, but upon the continuity of the Covenant, and the divine command that infants should receive the sign and seal of the Covenant in the Old Testament dispensation.

(3) It may be objected that we have no way of knowing whether or not infants are regenerate; in other words, whether or not they are members of Christ's mystical body. But it must be borne in mind, as has been expanded elsewhere in these pages, that even in the case of adults, baptism is not administered only to those who are regenerate. The person administering the rite is not able to know, infallibly, who *are* regenerate, and is not called upon to do so. Rather, he is required to insist upon, and be given, an intelligent and credible confession of faith. He is not required to, nor can he, go any further than that. Nevertheless, the grounds for infant baptism are uniquely established on the certainty of the divine command, and not on the uncertainty of individual regeneration.

(4) It may be objected that infants cannot understand the meaning of the rite of baptism. This is quite true, but it must not be inferred from this that infants do not derive any benefit from it. The same objection would be true concerning circumcision; but if we object to this we call into doubt the wisdom and grace of God, who instituted the rite for infants. The same objection, if valid, would apply to Christ's blessing little infants in His arms. Indeed, if we ponder this objection we must see that it rests upon the unworthy assumption that all blessing is contingent upon conscious understanding of its import, on our part. But we need only to refer to a very homely example to see how untrue this assumption is. It would surely be untrue to say that it is of no advantage to a child for it to be born and brought up and nurtured

in a Christian family, and yet the infant is not aware of this benefit.

D. A. Dunkerley, a pastor of a Presbyterian church in Florida, wrote the following, relating to infant baptism: ''Until they believe, the baptism is a sign and seal of salvation offered and it is meaningful whether the child becomes a Christian or not. ... When the child believes, then it becomes a sign not only of salvation offered, but salvation offered and received and effectually applied.''

But further considering whether there can be any benefit derived by the infant, we obtain some light on the subject from the Old Testament parallel relating to circumcision. And we may be sure that God would not expose His holy ordinances to contempt *then*, and be more careful that they may be more profitably used *now*. Some light therefore is to be obtained from the apostle Paul's discussion in Rom.3: 1, 2 — ''What advantage then hath the Jew? or what profit is there of circumcision?'' And answering his own question he says ''Much every way''. Then he proceeds to give his reasons: ''chiefly, because that unto them were committed the oracles of God'' (which contain God's Covenant). Being in the Christian Church is parallel to being a Jew, implies Paul, and the benefits are parallel.

Quite apart from the benefit to the *infant*, much good is received from it by the parents themselves. This is evident in the case of circumcision as we have it in Deut.4: 37. It is a great source of comfort and blessing for them to recognise in the seal the evidence that, not only do *they* cherish their children and long for their eternal blessing, but that the God from whom such blessing would proceed has indicated *His* interest in them also. Their admittance into church membership has a comforting and encouraging significance for parents who see them in God's appointed place of blessing, and who are stirred up thereby the more earnestly to pray for them, because God's Covenant of Grace provides arguments for their pleadings. But also, on account of their concern for their children, and their awareness of their dependence upon God's Covenant for any hoped-for blessing, this stirs up their hearts to be more sincerely holy, and to keep in with God, as it were; to educate their children with more care and watchfulness, realising that they are *God*'s children as well as *theirs*.

(5) It may be felt that it is an argument against infant baptism

that so many who were baptised in infancy have grown up to be disinterested in the Christian faith, and evidently without saving faith. But again it must be said that this sad and undeniable fact is also true of adults who have been baptised as adults and who have shown themselves later to be unbelievers. Too often those who are beneficiaries of this institution of grace rest upon the institution rather than upon God whose administration it is.

(6) It has been objected also that the paedobaptist argument drawn from the Old Testament rite of circumcision is not valid because of the great discrepancy that exists between circumcision and baptism. Perhaps the main force of this objection is contained in the fact that circumcision was only administered to males whereas baptism is administered to males *and* females. But the restriction to males in the case of circumcision was the divine institution and not therefore for us to question, but the extension of the Covenant sign and seal to females in the Christian era is entirely in keeping with the expansion of privilege revealed in the New Testament economy. It is one of the glories of the Gospel message that there is now in Christ Jesus no longer male nor female, just as there is no longer Jew nor Gentile, bond nor free.

But as discussed more fully elsewhere, the administering of baptism to infants in the New Testament economy stands in the same vital relation as the administering of circumcision to infants in the Old Testament economy.

(7) It is also sometimes objected that it is inconsistent to allow infants to participate in one sacrament — baptism — and not to allow them to participate in the other — the Lord's Supper. They say that under the Old Testament economy infants received the sign of circumcision and partook of the Passover feast of the paschal lamb; so why should they not participate in the corresponding sacraments in the New Testament economy, baptism and the Lord's Supper? But paedobaptists say they should receive baptism but *not* the Lord's Supper. Is this not inconsistent? Whereas the Baptists are consistent by not administering *either* rite to infants.

There is a fallacy however in this argument with respect to the supposition made in connection with the Passover. There is no evidence that infants partook of the Passover feast, and indeed it would be unreasonable to think that they did. Meat is not suitable food for infants, who, as we know, require a diet of milk at that age. In Ex.12: 21–28 we have instructions regarding the Passover ordinance, where we read "When your children shall say unto you, what mean ye by this service?" Clearly *these* children were old enough to understand the significance of the ordinance. In the same way paedobaptists would not refuse to admit to the Lord's table such children as had understanding and faith. The real differentiating factor is that the ground for infant baptism is other than faith exercised by the subject, whereas to partake of the Lord's Supper the recipient *must* have faith. Let us look at the distinctions between these two rites.

DISTINCTIONS BETWEEN BAPTISM AND THE LORD'S SUPPER

1. Baptism signifies and seals that which lies at the very inception of the state of salvation — union with Christ, cleansing from the pollution of sin and cleansing from the guilt of sin. It *signifies* what an infant *may* possess (as well as an adult) and what a person *must* possess in order to be a Christian and be in a state of salvation.

2. The Lord's Supper, on the other hand, signifies something that is consequent upon the state of salvation. The two central features of the Lord's Supper are commemoration and communion. The notions of remembrance, communion and discerning the Lord's body, are of such a nature that they necessitate conscious, intelligent understanding on the part of the participant; and for this reason, infants, not being capable of such spiritual and mental exercises, are not qualified for participating. For the reasons stated elsewhere, the things signified by baptism, on the other hand, do not necessarily involve intelligent understanding on the part of the participant, in the case of infants, and consequently baptism may be administered to such.

3. Baptism *represents* something that is performed in an individual once only, whereas the Lord's Supper represents what is constantly repeated in the life of that individual. For this reason the Lord's Supper is to be received frequently.

4. As we consider the elements appointed by God for these two sacraments we see how appropriate they are. Baptism is

associated with the notion of washing with water. How appropriate and necessary this is even in respect of an infant, in the earliest stages of its life! However, when we consider the partaking of bread and wine, in the case of the Lord's Supper, we can detect something that is incongruous with early infancy.

Summing up. Baptism *represents* the incorporating of the person baptised into the mystical body of Christ. It is the rite which *signifies* initiation. The Lord's Supper *represents* the abiding responsibility of, and provision for, those who are already members of Christ's mystical body. It is the rite of edification.

REQUIREMENTS FOR INFANT BAPTISM TO BE VALIDLY ADMINISTERED

Before leaving the subject of infant baptism, a particular aspect of it would seem to require clarification. We have considered reasons for asserting the Scriptural warrant for infant baptism, but in conclusion we must consider what are the circumstances and necessary requirements, applicable to any one instance, which would render the baptism of an infant *valid* in accordance with the reasoning already presented.

In other words what we are now to consider is the objection made by some, that the whole procedure of infant baptism seems to be so automatic as to appear to allow *any* infant to be baptised. Our present objective therefore is to attempt to clear up any uncertainty in this area, and to satisfy genuine misgivings arising from abuse of the rite.

The subject has been partially touched on already, but the implications are so important, and mistakes resulting from a misunderstanding of the Biblical teaching so fraught with danger, that I consider a review of the whole matter, and the introduction of some hitherto unstated principles, to be fully justified, in order to complete the overall teaching relating to infant baptism as represented in this treatise.

Perhaps it may help us, in order to see clearly the issues before us, to set down the separate *parties*, or *factors* involved in any case where the rite of baptism is administered. Baptism, whether administered to adults or infants is a church ordinance. It is something that the Head of the Church has ordained or commanded, and His Church is the instrument that He has appointed, and made responsible, for the administering of this ordinance.

This provides us therefore with the first requirement or condition for *valid* baptism — it must be carried out by a true Christian church. This is the *first* of the parties involved — the church.

The *next* party to be considered is the one administering the rite of baptism, the minister of the particular church in connection with which the rite is being observed.

The *third* party involved comprises the parents of the infant (in the case of infant baptism), or the adult person professing faith in the Lord Jesus Christ, in the case of an adult person being baptised.

The *fourth* party, in the case of infant baptism, is the infant being baptised.

As we are here particularly concerned with the administration of the sacrament of baptism to an infant, we will consider in turn the four parties involved, as mentioned above, associated with infant baptism.

First of all it is important that we are quite clear as to what constitutes *a true Christian church*, and it is for this reason that a whole chapter of this treatise has been devoted to this one subject. I do not propose therefore to occupy much space in considering this subject here but will limit myself to a few features which are particularly relevant to the subject before us.

We must remember that the Church is represented by local congregations in different places throughout the world, and those congregations, generally speaking, are mixed bodies. They consist not only of converted persons, but of unconverted persons also. We find many references to this situation in the Scriptures. Particularly important in this respect are the addresses of the Lord Jesus Christ to the churches of Asia as recorded in the Book of the Revelation, chapters 2 and 3.

We must further bear in mind the variation in the government of local churches. At this point I will quote from that godly Bishop of Liverpool, John Charles Ryle. Referring to the New Testament churches he writes:

"What kind of governments some churches had it is impossible to say positively. We read of officers who were called angels, of bishops, of deacons, of elders, of pastors, of teachers, of evangelists, of prophets, of helps, of governments. But the particulars about most of these officers are kept from us by the Spirit of God. As to the standard of doctrine and practice in the churches, we have the fullest and most distinct information. But as to government and outward ceremonies, the information given to us is strikingly small."

Again quoting from Ryle on the same subject and as a deduction from the foregoing, he writes:

"No visible church on earth has a right to say: 'We are the true church, and except men belong to our communion they cannot be saved' — Furthermore, no visible church has a right to say: 'We alone have the true form of worship, the true church government, the true way of administering the sacraments.' "

These would seem to be particularly salutary remarks, coming, as they do, from an honoured servant of the Church. Reference has already been made in this treatise, in the section dealing with the Church, to the notorious disagreement amongst God-honouring people, regarding such matters as church government and outward ceremonies, but happily, these things do not constitute the marks of a true church.

And again quoting from Ryle:—

"No visible church is in a sound and healthy state, which has not the marks we see in all the New Testament churches. A church in which the Bible is *not* the standard of faith and practice, — a church in which repentance, faith and holiness, are *not* prominently put forward as essential to salvation, — a church in which forms, and ceremonies, and ordinances not commanded in the Bible, are the chief things urged upon the attention of the members, — such a church is in a very diseased and unsatisfactory condition."

In this way Ryle acknowledges, and to a certain extent explains, the variety which we see to-day in the spectrum of the local representations of the Christian Church, at the same time indicating the importance of looking for certain essential basic elements which should always be present in any local congregation.

"There are churches", continues Ryle, "in which Jesus Christ's

Gospel is buried. — There are churches in which a man may hear God's service performed — and never hear of 'repentance towards God, faith toward Christ', and the work of the Holy Ghost. — Such are the Armenian and Greek churches, and such, above all in corruption, is the Church of Rome. To belong to such churches brings tremendous peril upon anybody's soul.''

A true church, one which may be considered to be a fit instrument for administering the rite of Christian baptism, I will call a Gospel church because the spiritual significance of Christian baptism is so intimately associated with the message of the Gospel. But in the light of the foregoing we must come to the conclusion that there are certain churches, which cannot be called Gospel churches, which perform the ceremony of the rite, but due to their corrupt constitution such a carrying out of the rite cannot be regarded as valid Christian baptism.

A church may have many blemishes, but we must be able to discern in its constitution certain marks which show it to be a Gospel church, otherwise we cannot regard such a church to be a fit instrument for administering the rite.

We will take, as an example of this situation, a local church within the Roman Catholic communion, and this we may consider as being representative of any such church coming within the same category.

In this connection I propose to quote from James Henley Thornwell, a well accredited American theologian (1812–1862). It may perhaps contribute to a proper assessment of the importance of the subject before us to mention that some measure of disagreement on it existed between Dr. Thornwell and the highly esteemed Dr. Charles Hodge (1797–1878). Both men being professors in American theological seminaries. In my opinion the ground upon which Hodge based his views is unsubstantial, stressing as it does the prime importance of the baptismal formula to be used, rather than the evangelical constitution of the church.

The occasion of the treatise by Thornwell from which I quote, arose from a judgment made by the Presbyterian General Assembly meeting in 1845, in which Dr. Thornwell took a leading part. This judgment was opposed (it is understood) by Dr. Hodge. This treatise (from which I quote) was Dr. Thornwell's response to Dr. Hodge.

Quite obviously it would be inappropriate here to do more than touch on the views there expressed, but it is hoped that this somewhat scanty treatment will nevertheless bring out the way the subject was approached, and at the same time underline the importance and significance of the settled judgment arrived at by the General Assembly when it decided that the ceremony of baptism performed by the Roman Catholic Church is not valid. This judgment provides us with a very valuable guideline to help us to find our way through this rather difficult ecclesiastical territory.

Dr. Thornwell states that the General Assembly ''denied the validity of Popish baptism'' because ''the ordinance itself was so corrupted in its constituent elements — its matter and its form — that it could not be treated as the institution of Christ, and the Papal communion, as an organised body, being destitute of some of the indispensable marks of a true church, could not be recognised in that character''.

''To the question 'What constitutes the validity of baptism?' the reply obviously is 'The conformity of any rite with the definition of baptism which may be collected from the Scriptures and justified by them'. The validity of a sacrament does not depend upon any effects which its produces, but upon its nature: — and whatever *coincides* with the appointment of Christ, so as to be essentially the same ordinance which *He* instituted, must be received as bearing *His* sanction.''

''When the Assembly, therefore, decided that Popish baptism is not valid, it intended to assert that what in that corrupt communion is administered under the name of baptism is really a different instititution from the ordinance of Christ. Rome's ceremony does not answer to a just definition of the Christian sacrament.''

In concluding his treatise Dr. Thornwell states:— ''The institute of Rome is neither a sign nor a seal, however she may apply these epithets to it; and even if it were, as she has introduced another gospel and another scheme of salvation, she must necessarily have introduced another baptism. — When the truths of the Covenant are discarded, its signs lose their efficacy and its seals their power.''

The foregoing will no doubt give some acknowledgment of the

important role to be played by the *church* in the administration of the rite of baptism. We will now move on to consider the next of the four parties referred to earlier, namely the one administering the rite of baptism.

It is important, particularly in connection with the subject before us, that we recognise two distinct aspects relating to *the officiating minister*. He is first of all to be a duly accredited minister who is lawfully commissioned to dispense the mysteries of Christ. The first requirement is inevitably related to a true Christian church. I do not need to elaborate this point, but just to illustrate it by taking an extreme example — It would clearly be unacceptable for the rite to be administered by a heathen priest in a church building which is normally used for the Christian ministry. That is one aspect of the person administering the rite. There must be some evidence and acknowledgment of his declared loyalty to the true Christian church — to a Gospel church. But secondly, we must recognise that as well as being one holding public office, he is also a private individual.

The question arises here as to what is required of such an officiating minister when considered as a private individual. Do we insist on him being a born-again man, a true Christian? This question can best be answered, I believe, when we recall a principle touched on elsewhere in this treatise, namely the fact that no man, however spiritually minded and discerning he may be, can finally determine who is, and who is not, a Christian. Only God can do this. So we must not make this personal quality a criterion when judging the fitness of a person to perform this rite.

Furthermore, we find many examples in the Scriptures of God employing ungodly and heathen nations and kings for the carrying out of His purposes. For example, concerning Cyrus, the heathen king of Persia, God says to His people Israel:- "Thus saith the LORD, thy redeemer, and He — that saith of Cyrus, He is My shepherd, and shall perform all My pleasure: even saying to Jerusalem, Thou shalt be built; and to the temple, Thy foundation shall be laid" (Isaiah 44: 24, 28)

My conclusion therefore is that we must not insist on a particular quality in the person administering the rite, but we *must* insist that the rite is carried out by a person who is lawfully commissioned by what I have referred to as a Gospel church, and also carried out in accordance with the formularies of that church. By insisting on these requirements it can be seen that when the church is in a spiritually healthy state, and is exercising Gospel discipline, it will be vigilant in its examination of its ministers, looking for evidence of the rebirth. But on the other hand when the church is in a decadent condition, and discipline is slack, it is quite likely that many of its ministers will not have experienced the new birth, and their personal walk may not be such as "becometh the Gospel of Christ" (Phil.1:27).

Notwithstanding the possibility of variations in personal qualities, corresponding to such variations in the spiritual vitality of the church, provided that the official qualifications referred to above are fully complied with, the spiritual state of the officiating minister will not invalidate the rite. If the validity of the rite depended upon whether or not the minister is born again, which cannot be infallibly determined by men, then the position of the subject of baptism would be quite untenable.

Next we consider the third party involved in this rite, namely the *parents* of the infant to be baptised. What qualification, if any, is required in the case of the parents in order that the baptism administered may be valid?

I do not need to spend much time on this aspect because it brings before us the subject and discussion of this whole chapter on infant baptism. The justification for the validity of infant baptism is found in the terms of the Covenant of Grace. Those who are the primary participators in the Covenant are the parents, and the infant is brought under the terms of the Covenant for the sake of the parents, who themselves should have received the sign and seal of the Covenant, thereby giving evidence of being God's Covenant people — of being Christians.

The infant, together with the parents, being all within the terms of the Covenant, are not in the world, under the dominion of Satan, but within the protection of the church, and so federally holy (1 Cor.7: 14). A further refinement comes in at this point, sanctioned by the Word of God. The requirement of the Covenant is met even if only one of the parents is a Christian (see page 62). "The unbelieving husband is sanctified by the wife (that is, constituted federally holy by the wife being a Christian), and the unbelieving wife is sanctified by the husband: else were your children unclean (federally unholy); but now are they holy'' (1 Cor.7:14). (See also Westminster Confession of Faith, chap.XXVIII Section IV). So we conclude that at least one of the parents, whether Jew or Gentile, must be a Christian, trusting in the saving work of the Lord Jesus Christ in order that the baptism administered may be deemed to be valid.

We should, I think, in order to satisfy all possible circumstances, consider the situation where an infant is baptised on the basis of its parents' Christian profession, which profession in later years has reason to be called into question. What is the child's position *then*? Does this subsequent uncertainty about the genuineness of its parents' profession threaten the validity of its baptism?

The answer to this question is to be found in the constitution of the Gospel church, which we have just been considering. The rite of Christian baptism was administered by a person lawfully commissioned by a Gospel church. Furthermore, before this was done, the parents gave a credible profession of faith in Christ, and promised obedience to Him. As we have observed several times already, this is as far as the officers of the church *can* go, and are *required* to go. On that basis the infant was baptised, and that baptism was recognised by the church as valid. It would be quite untenable therefore, for that validity to be called into question, in later years, on account of the officers of the church being misled by the parents' profession of faith. It was accepted as genuine. The validity of the baptism of the infant is not suspended perilously on the genuineness of its parents' Christian profession, which will not be infallibly known until the Day of Judgment. Rather, we may be assured, for the reasons given, that baptism administered under *such* circumstances is indeed valid.

Finally, coming to the fourth party concerned in the rite, we consider the *subject* of the baptism, namely the infant. What requirements are to be laid down in this case, to ensure that the baptism administered is valid?

First we can say, simply, that one of the parents of the infant (if not both) must be a true Christian. We can also include infants who are adopted by such parents. We have Scriptural warrant for this in the case of God's commands to Abraham in Gen.17:9–13 & 23 regarding administering the sign and seal to his seed, and not only *his* but also those in his household.

Negatively, it is not required that the infant be elect — no man could know that. Nor is it required that the infant shall, later, become a Christian — none could tell that. The only requirement, or qualification, as far as the infant is concerned, is that which has been stated above.

To sum up therefore, the factors governing infant baptism which shall determine whether or not it is valid are these four:

(1) The church where the rite is administered must be a Gospel church, in whose constitution it is possible to discern certain marks which show it to be such.

(2) The officiating minister must be one who has been lawfully commissioned to dispense the mysteries of Christ in accordance with the formularies of a true Gospel church. He must give some evidence, and acknowledgment, of his declared loyalty to such a church.

(3) At least one of the parents of the infant to be baptised must be a true Christian.

(4) The infant to be baptised must be the natural seed or the adopted seed of its parents, one parent at least being a Christian, as in (3).

★ ★ ★

"I beseech you, brethren, by the name of our Lord Jesus Christ, that ye all speak the same thing, and that there be no divisions among you; but that ye be perfectly joined together in the same mind and in the same judgment."

1 Cor.1:10.

THE MODE OF BAPTISM

We now come to consider that much debated subject of how the rite of baptism should be administered, and whether a particular method of applying water, or of relating a person to water, is of the essence of the symbolism. As mentioned earlier, John Murray's book "Infant Baptism" has been used very freely in the preparation of this section. It is evident from this book that it represents the so called paedobaptist interpretation of the Scriptural teaching on this subject. Nevertheless the points raised in his analysis are open to clear scrutiny and verification and merit careful consideration.

Inevitably, as we come to look at this aspect of our subject, we will be looking at the meanings of words, such as the meaning of the original Greek word which is translated by the word "baptise". What we will be concerned to discover is not what these words *can* mean but whether in Scripture usage they *always* have that one and only meaning. I think it is appreciated that with regard to this subject there are two principal interpretations of the Scriptural teaching on baptism, one as represented by this treatise and referred to as the paedobaptist view, the word being derived from the Greek word for infant. The other interpretation is referred to as the Baptist view, which contends that the *mode* of baptism is of the essence of the symbolism used, and that since "baptise" *means* to immerse, baptism is not properly administered by any other mode.

The Baptist argument rests mainly upon *two contentions*. Firstly that the Greek word BAPTIZO *means* to immerse, and secondly that passages such as the following, plainly imply that the death and resurrection of Christ provide us with the pattern for immersion *in*, and emergence *from*, the water.

"Know ye not, that so many of us as were baptised into Jesus Christ were baptised into His death? Therefore we are buried with Him by baptism into death: that like as Christ was raised up from the dead by the glory of the Father, even so we also should walk in newness of life. For if we have been planted together in the likeness of His death, we shall be also in the likeness of His resurrection: knowing this, that our old man is crucified with Him, that the body of sin might be destroyed, that henceforth we should not serve sin" (Rom.6: 3–6).

"In whom also ye are circumcised with the circumcision made without hands, in putting off the body of the sins of the flesh by the circumcision of Christ: buried with Him in baptism, wherein also ye are risen with Him through the faith of the operation of God, who hath raised Him from the dead" (Col.2: 11, 12).

MEANING OF CRUCIAL WORDS IN OLD TESTAMENT

In view of the fundamental position of these two contentions in relation to the Baptist interpretation it is most important that we look at each in turn. First of all we will examine a number of cases where the original word translated "baptise" or its derivatives, have been used, to see whether the contexts throw any light upon the basic meaning of the words. In doing this, we will first of all look at the Old Testament Scriptures, and afterwards we will look at the New Testament. In carrying out this particular study it is important that we should remember the fact that the whole of the Old Testament was translated from the original Hebrew into Greek about 280 years before the Christian era. This work was thought to have been carried out by 70 translators, hence the name given to the translation as the "Septuagint". Most of the quotations of the Old Testament which are given in the New Testament are apparently from that version. Jesus would have been familiar with that version.

In the Septuagint the Greek word BAPTIZO occurs very infrequently. One case is found in 2 Kings 5: 14. It translates the Hebrew word TABAL which means "to dip" or "to be moist with".

It is the Greek word BAPTO which occurs *most* frequently in the Septuagint, occurring about 17 times. In most cases it translates TABAL, just as BAPTIZO does in 2 Kings 5: 14. TABAL certainly means "to dip" and so also does its Greek rendering BAPTO. BAPTO may *also* refer to immersion, as it does when used in Lev.11: 32, to translate the Hebrew word BO. In Ps.68: 23, 24 BAPTO has been used to translate the Hebrew word MACHATS, meaning "to smite through", or "to dash". The question which we must ask here is whether TABAL and BAPTO *necessarily* and *invariably* refer to immersion and that they therefore always *mean* "to immerse".

We have seen that these two words *can,* and sometimes *do,* refer to immersion, but my purpose is to show that they do not *invariably* refer to immersion; so that when we come across either word in the Scriptures we are not able to say that it *must* refer to immersion. It may not do so. Let us look at this.

In Lev.14: 6 we are given details of the ritual laid down in the Law of God for the cleansing of a leper and in verse 51 similar details are given for the cleansing of a house in which the plague of leprosy had appeared. The living bird was to be dipped in the blood of the bird that was slain. The Hebrew word for "dipped" is TABAL and the Greek word is BAPTO. Now here is a case where BAPTO is used to denote an action that cannot be construed as immersion. So we must conclude that it does not *mean* immersion. This is not its *invariable* meaning. Furthermore, because of this conclusion, when it *does* refer to immersion we cannot *know* this from the meaning of the word. In order to determine its meaning in any particular case we must do so from other considerations, relating to the context. It is of interest that in the above Scripture the live bird was to be baptised *into the blood* of the slain bird. So we can conclude that even the expression to "baptise into" does not mean "to immerse", and the preposition "into" does not add any force to the argument that BAPTO means "to immerse".

In Lev.14: 15, 16 we read of how the priest is required to pour oil into the palm of his own left hand: "And the priest shall dip his right finger in the oil that is in his left hand". The word used for "dip" here is the same Hebrew word TABAL meaning "to dip" or "to be moist with". The Greek word in the Septuagint is again

BAPTO, so once again we see that it cannot here refer to immersion.

In Ruth 2: 14 we read of Boaz saying to Ruth "dip thy morsel in the vinegar". It would be unreasonable to think of this "dipping" referring to "immersion". It must mean "to dip" in the normal sense of that word. So here again BAPTO does *not* refer to immersion.

In 1 Sam.14: 27 we read of how Jonathan dipped "the end of his rod that was in his hand .. in an honeycomb". It would be unreasonable to imagine that the rod was immersed in the honeycomb; it must surely mean "dipped". So here is another instance where BAPTO does *not* refer to immersion.

We may reasonably deduce from the foregoing examples that we *cannot* assume that in all the other cases where BAPTO is used it means "immersion", as for example in Ex.12: 22; Lev.4: 6, 17; Lev.9: 9; Numbers 19: 18; Deut.33: 24. There is nothing in the Hebrew word used, nor in the contexts of the passages concerned, which requires the sense of "immersion".

With reference to the episode described in 2 Kings 5 concerning Naaman, and in particular in verse 14, there is no evidence which can be derived from the terms used in Hebrew or Greek, or from the details of the narrative, to prove that he immersed himself.

With reference to the episode described in Joshua 3 relating to the crossing of the Jordan, and in particular in verse 15, this cannot be adduced to prove that the priests' feet were immersed in the water. We are told that their feet were "dipped" or "baptised" in the brink of the river. It is of course possible that their feet were immersed in the water, but there is nothing to prove this to have been the case. The dipping (literally) of the their feet in the brink of the river is all that is necessary to satisfy the terms used both in Hebrew and in Greek. In verse 13 we are told that when "the soles of the feet of the priests . . . shall 'rest' in the waters" — the waters should "stand upon an heap". The kind of contact with the water mentioned in verse 13 satisfies the terms of verse 15. The "dipping" in verse 15 must have the same meaning as the resting of the soles of the feet in verse 13.

In all the passages considered so far there is only the case of Lev.11: 32 where BAPTO clearly refers to an action which seems fairly clearly to involve immersion.

To conclude our consideration of the meaning of the word BAPTO in the Old Testament we will look at two further Scriptures which are found in the Book of Daniel, 4: 33 and 5: 21. The body of Nebuchadnezzar was wet with the dew of heaven – or bathed with the dew of heaven. In these instances the Greek word BAPTO translates an Aramaic verb, which occurs also in Dan.4: 12, 20 and 22; but only in Dan.4: 33 and 5: 21 is it translated by the word BAPTO. It could mean that his body was dipped in the dew of heaven, but it seems to be much more reasonable to assume that the thought expressed is that his body was drenched or bathed with the dew of heaven. On the other hand the expression could carry a weaker meaning, indicating that his body was simply moist with the dew of heaven. In any case, the thought cannot be adjusted to the notion that his body was literally immersed in the dew of heaven. So here again we have an instance of the use of the term BAPTO in a sense other than that of immersion. From the foregoing instances in the Old Testament we see that there is nothing to imply that in any of them, with the exception of Lev.11: 32, immersion was employed or even suggested, and we are therefore compelled to conclude that the term BAPTO does not *mean* immersion.

MEANING OF CRUCIAL WORDS IN NEW TESTAMENT

We will now turn our attention to the meaning of terms used in the New Testament. Here we find that the word BAPTO recedes into the background and the word BAPTIZO comes into the foreground. The former occurs only four times (Luke 16: 24; John 13: 26(twice) and Rev.19: 13) whereas the latter occurs nearly 80 times. As well as the word BAPTIZO, the associated substantive BAPTISMA (baptism) occurs about 20 times. Our procedure will be the same as for the Old Testament in that we will not be concerned whether these terms *may* be used to denote an action performed by immersion, but rather whether they *mean* immersion *always* and could not properly denote an action performed by any other mode.

We will first of all look at the tradition of the elders of the Jews of washing their hands before taking food. We find this in Matt.15: 2; Mark 7: 2–5 and Luke 11:38.

It appears from certain Jewish writings and Christian authorities (Lightfoot and Edersheim) that there were two ways of washing the hands before eating, namely by dipping the hands in water, or by pouring water over the hands. In Matthew and Mark the Greek word used to wash is NIPTO meaning to wash or wet; but in Luke the word used is BAPTIZO.

In Luke 11: 37 we have a narrative of how a Pharisee invited Jesus to dine with him, and we are told that the Pharisee marvelled because Jesus "had not first baptised Himself before dinner". (v.38). It is evident to common sense that the Pharisee could not have expected Jesus to have completely immersed Himself before dining.

So here we have evidence that the word BAPTIZO *can* be used in referring to an action which does not involve being immersed. From the three references to the Jewish tradition of washing before meals, mentioned above, we see that the action of washing the hands by dipping them in water, or more probably by pouring water upon them, can be called baptism. It is interesting to notice that in the margin of the 1887 revision of the Authorised Version of the Bible a note indicates that there is a variant in the manuscript authority. Some manuscripts use the word BAPTIZO in Mark 7: 4 whereas others use the word RHAN which means "sprinkle".

It would appear that there is a difference between the washings of verses 3 and 4 in Mark Chapter 7. Verse 3 refers to the washing of hands before partaking of a meal, as already discussed; but verse 4 refers to washing on return from the market, the place where food is sold. This latter washing is referring to ceremonial washing, as is evident by Mark enumerating a number of articles that had to be ceremonially cleansed, including tables (given in the A.V. margin as beds). Mark seems to be explaining, in this chapter, for the benefit of his Gentile readers, the Jewish practice relating to these washings. The reference is not to washing for the sake of cleanliness, but for ritual or ceremonial purposes, it means to wash symbolically as a religious rite. In this connection the reference should be noted in Numbers 8: 5–7 to God's command to Moses to "sprinkle water of purifying upon them".

This leads us naturally to look at Heb.9: 10–23. In verse 10 we have the expression "divers washings" (the Greek BAPTISMOS), or "divers baptisms", alluding to various symbolical purifications or lustrations of the Old Testament which were for the cleansing of the body from ceremonial defilement but not the soul from moral guilt.

The significance of this passage, as it bears upon our present investigation, is that the "divers baptisms" of verse 10 must surely include the lustrations expressly referred to in the succeeding verses. In these verses a contrast is being drawn between the relative inefficacy of the ritual ordinances of the Levitical economy and the transcendent efficacy and perfection of Christ's purificatory and expiatory work. In this sustained contrast every lustratory rite that comes within the apostle's purview must be included in the "divers baptisms" of verse 10, one of which is expressly stated in verse 13 to have been performed by sprinkling. And so it is evident that a lustratory rite performed by sprinkling can be called a baptism.

In verse 19 also, reference is made to sprinkling, and again in verse 21, reference is made to the sprinkling of "the tabernacle, and all the vessels of the ministry" (See Ex. 24: 6–8). These ordinances are expressly stated in verse 23 to be for purification and are referred to in verse 10 as "divers baptisms". We must conclude, therefore, that the word "baptism" refers here to an action that can be performed by sprinkling, and cannot *mean* (exclusively) immersion. Moreover, we know from the Old Testament that several of the Levitical lustrations, in addition to those mentioned in this chapter, were performed by sprinkling. See, for instance, Lev.14: 7, 16 & 51; Lev.16: 19, Num.8: 7; 19: 18, 19.

The significance of sprinkling is shown clearly by the fact that when the high priest went into the holiest of all, once a year, on the great day of atonement, he sprinkled the blood of the sin-offerings seven times before the mercy seat and upon the mercy seat, as we have it in Lev.16: 14, 15. That this sprinkling had reference to cleansing appears from verse 19 of that chapter. The Hebrew words used for the act of sprinkling are ZARAQ and NAZAH. Ezek.36: 25 indicates as clearly as any text in the Old Testament the purificatory significance of sprinkling, and the adequacy of sprinkling as a mode of ceremonial purification.

If the Baptist argument were to be valid, it would be necessary for the "divers baptisms" of Heb.9: 10 to be restricted to those lustratory rites which were performed by immersion, and would have to exclude the most significant lustratory rites and actions of the old economy, incorporating sprinkling, which of course would be a quite untenable supposition. This passage in the epistle to the Hebrews therefore provides us with an instance where the word "baptism" (BAPTISMOS) denotes actions which do not involve immersion.

We will now consider the use of the word "baptism" in connection with the events on the Day of Pentecost. Quite clearly the statement in Matt.3: 11 cannot mean "He shall immerse you with the Holy Ghost, and with fire". We find that the baptism with the Holy Spirit is referred to in terms that are quite contrary to the idea of immersion, and in fact preclude it. In Acts 1: 8 the Holy Spirit is represented as "coming upon" the disciples. The Greek word used conveys the idea of "coming down upon". In Acts 2: 17 & 33 the Holy Spirit is represented as having been "poured out". In Acts 10: 44 and 11: 15 He is represented as having "fallen upon" the persons concerned. It is very evident that the terms in each case are those of affusion and not of immersion, but this affusion is called "baptism".

Furthermore, the "baptism with fire" received its symbolic fulfilment in the "cloven tongues like as of fire" that "sat upon each of" the disciples (see Acts 2: 3). This baptism with fire cannot be adjusted to the notion of immersion. But for the Baptist argument to be valid, that "baptism" *means* "immersion", the phenomena referred to in the "Acts" must involve immersion, which we know they did not. Furthermore the language of the Old Testament prophecies of these phenomena is in terms of "pouring out", "shedding forth" and "sprinkling" (see Prov.1: 23; Is.32: 15; Ezek.36: 25–27; Joel 2: 28).

RELEVANCE OF THE ACT OF SPRINKLING

Bearing in mind that our immediate objective is to determine whether or not the mode of baptism, as presented to us in the Scriptures, is immersion, and *only* immersion, we will go on now to consider the relevance of the *act of sprinkling*, as it appears in the Scriptures and whether it could be applied to the act of baptising.

Baptism symbolises, represents and seals, to the person baptised, the application of the blood of Christ, "the blood of sprinkling, that speaketh better things than that of Abel'' (Heb.12: 24). And see also Heb.9: 13, 14; 10: 22 and 1 Peter 1: 2. It would be strange if the baptism with water, which *represents* the sprinkling of the blood of Christ, could not properly, and most significantly, be performed by sprinkling. In this respect we must never lose sight of the fact that, according to Scripture, cleansing from the guilt of sin is adequately and effectively administered, symbolically, by the mode of sprinkling, no less than by the modes of affusion and immersion, as we have already seen.

The Westminster Directory for the Public Worship of God makes the following statement in the section dealing with the sacrament of baptism: ''The water, in baptism, representeth and signifieth both the blood of Christ, which taketh away all guilt of sin, original and actual; and the sanctifying virtue of the Spirit of Christ against the dominion of sin, and the corruption of our sinful nature.''

Sufficient evidence has been presented above to show that in the usage of the New Testament, BAPTIZO does not *mean* to immerse. It *can* be used with reference to the acts of immersion, affusion and sprinkling. This corroborates the conclusions which were reached, in a similar way, in our consideration of the Old Testament Scriptures.

OTHER SIGNIFICANT NEW TESTAMENT SCRIPTURES

Nevertheless, in order to clear any uncertainties remaining we must look particularly at some other New Testament Scriptures which have been appealed to on both sides of the discussion.

The first Scripture which we will look at is 1 Cor.10: 1, 2 ''all our fathers were . . . baptised unto Moses''. Now if ''baptism'' means ''immersion'' then the children of Israel would have to be regarded as having been immersed in the cloud and in the sea. But we know that they were not immersed in the sea, they passed through the sea on dry ground, and the reference to the cloud is surely to the pillar of cloud that went before them by day. A cloud that did not come upon them and into which they did not enter. So we see that the word BAPTIZO is used here with reference to events which did not involve immersion in any way. So we can conclude that here again the word BAPTIZO does not *mean* to immerse.

Another Scripture which we must look at is that relating to the occasion when Philip met an Ethiopian eunuch as we have it in Acts 8: 26–40.

Those who have argued *against* the mode of immersion have sometimes appealed to this Scripture in support of their view by arguing that since the area was desert it would be improbable, if not impossible, to find enough water for the purpose of immersion. But this is not a valid argument. It cannot be *proved* that the Ethiopian was not immersed by Philip.

However, it becomes equally necessary to show that the Baptist appeal to this text, to prove the case for immersion, is also indefensible. Is it not said that both *Philip and the eunuch went down* into the water and that *they came up* out of the water? (vv.38,39) Is not immersion implied by the prepositions "into" and "out of"? But immersion cannot be established by such expressions. It would mean that Philip immersed *himself,* as well as the eunuch. Such supposition is therefore seen to be quite unreasonable. So we see that this passage does not *prove* immersion. The expressions "they went down both into the water" and they both came "up out of the water" are satisfied by the thought that they both went down *to* the water, stood on the brink, or stepped into the edge, and that Philip baptised the eunuch by scooping up the water and pouring it, or sprinkling it on him. What the actual mode was, we are not able to determine from this Scripture.

JOHN THE BAPTIST

The very subject which we have before us, baptism, demands that we give some consideration to the unique and outstanding figure of John the Baptist; the last of the Old Testament prophets, who broke the silence of heaven since the days of Malachi. He stands at the same point of transition, in the economy of God, as did the Lord Jesus Christ when here in the flesh. This was a transition from the Old Testatment economy to the New Testament economy; from the Jewish era, when the sign and seal of the Covenant was circumcision, to the era when baptism was the sign and seal. Not surprisingly, therefore, we find, to a certain extent, a measure of overlapping of the two economies. Intimations of this are recognised in John 3: 22–26. In verse 22 we read that Jesus and

His disciples had come into the land of Judea "and baptised" (but in John 4: 2 we are told that this was done by His disciples). In verse 23 we are told about John the Baptist baptising. So both our Lord's disciples and John were baptising people at the same time, some came to Jesus and some to John. Their baptisms were the same, and they were united in heart and purpose.

In verse 25 we are told that there arose a question between some of John's disciples and the Jews about purifying, which from the context can be seen to be referring to the rite of baptism; the symbolical meaning of washing with water being put for the act itself. We are reminded by John "the evangelist" in the previous chapter (chap.2), verse 6, that the ceremonial washings were still being practised, including the washings required by the law of Moses. There were the washings from the plague of leprosy, symbolising the cleansing from the corruption and pollution of sin; also the washings of sanctification symbolised by the washing of the high priest, as we have it recorded for us in Lev.16: 4.

Some think that *symbolical washing* by baptism was then in use by the Jews, as an appendix to circumcision, and that it was in this way that Gentile proselytes were initiated into the Jewish religion (See proselyte-baptism, page 126). Whatever the particulars of the dispute may have been which is referred to in John 3: 25, it appears to have been related to some departure from the custom of the Jews in the baptism administered by John. We could conjecture what this might be, but this would be to no purpose. My chief purpose in this connection is to emphasise the Old Testament *purification* aspect of the baptism of John.

It seems to me that the little episode which we find recorded in the Acts of the Apostles, chapter 19, verses 1 to 7, but particularly verses 3 to 5; that this episode relates to this *very* subject, showing there to be a fundamental difference between John's baptism and that ordained by the Lord Jesus Christ.

The authoritative divine command for the institution of the ordinance of Christian baptism was given by the *risen* Christ, as recorded in Matt.28: 19, 20. There was no previous divine command to introduce the baptism of John, which leads us to the same conclusion that *that* baptism was a part of the Mosaic ceremonial law and of the same nature as the rite of circumcision administered to John the Baptist and to Jesus. No doubt the Jews remembered the prophecy of Ezekiel, foretelling the coming Messiah: "Then will I sprinkle clean water upon you, and ye shall be clean: from all your filthiness, and from all your idols, will I cleanse you" (Ez.36:25) They perhaps reasoned with themselves, that this sort of baptising was a distinctly *Messianic* act, something that related to the Old Testament lustrations, and so why was *this* man (John) administering such baptism? (see John 1: 25).

Having observed the nature of the baptism of John, we will now briefly consider the significance of the expressions used in connection with it. We read that John baptised *in* Jordan (Matt.3: 6 and Mark 1: 5) and *into* Jordan (Mark 1: 9). (But in the A.V. this is "in Jordan"). He also baptised *in* Aenon (John 3: 23).

We are concerned here to determine whether the record of John's baptism gives us infallible proof that he baptised by the mode of immersion. Although we have seen that John's baptism is not what we may call Christian baptism; nevertheless, if it could be proved that he practised immersion, it would have significance regarding the baptism instituted by the Lord Jesus Christ.

We can say at the outset that John *may* have practised baptism by immersion but the expressions used and the circumstances described do not *prove* that immersion was the mode used, nor does the choice of Jordan and Aenon as the places where he baptised. There are several other sufficient reasons why these places should have been chosen. There was a scarcity of water in the land, which was needed for other purposes. Water was needed by the large number of people and their animals. There were a number of such reasons why a good supply of water was needed, as well as for the purpose of baptism. So, we are not able to conclude that baptism was by immersion simply on account of the fact of there being a good supply of water available.

The expressions "in Jordan" and "into Jordan" do not prove immersion. The first may be nothing more than a designation of location, just as baptising in Aenon, or at Aenon. This is a name, which is nowhere else mentioned in Scripture, and its exact location is not known. Some think that it was the name of a city where there were many streams. The phrase is literally "— because there were many waters there", or "many streams of water". The expression "into Jordan" in Mark 1: 9, as for Acts 8: 26–40 referred to above, does not necessarily imply immersion.

It will be remembered that we have been examining a number of Scriptures, both in the Old Testament and in the New Testament to see if any positive evidence can be found that the original words used in the text mean exclusively to immerse. On the basis of the cases considered we are led to the conclusion that though the word BAPTIZO and its related words *can* be used to denote an action performed by immersion, yet they may also be used to denote an action that can be performed by other modes. Consequently the term BAPTIZO itself cannot be pleaded as an argument for the necessity of immersion as the *exclusive* mode of baptism.

TEACHING OF ROMANS CHAPTER 6

At the beginning of this section we set out to consider whether the mode of baptism *is of the essence of the symbolism.* The Baptists claim that it is, and that since the word for "baptise" means to immerse, baptism is not properly administered by any other mode. We have now concluded our consideration of this claim. But there is a second contention, made by those holding the Baptist position, and we must now proceed to consider this. This second contention is that such passages as Rom. 6: 3–6 and Col.2: 11, 12 plainly imply that the death and resurrection of Christ provide us with the pattern for immersion *in* and emergence *from,* the water.

We will concentrate on the passage in the sixth chapter of Paul's epistle to the Romans, as this is the one upon which most emphasis has been placed. But first of all let us be clear as to Paul's general purpose at this point. At the close of chapter 5 verses 20 & 21 Paul has said that "the law entered, that the offence might abound. But where sin abounded, grace did much more abound." This seemed to raise two possible queries. First, does this mean that the Law of God had no purpose? Second, does this mean the more one sins the more is the grace of God enhanced? In chapter 5 Paul has been handling the subject of justification. But at chapter 6 he pauses as it were, and deals with the second difficulty. "Shall we continue in sin, that grace may abound?" In chapter 7 he deals with the whole subject of the place and function of the Law in the economy of God. Then in chapter 8 he resumes the subject of justification; chapters 6 & 7 being a sort of interruption of the argument to deal with these two possible objections. It seems to be agreed by all, even Roman Catholics and others, that the fundamental doctrine contained in the passage referred to in the sixth chapter, is that of the believer's union with the Lord Jesus Christ. But as this passage has been interpreted in a number of different ways, we will pause to consider some of these interpretations.

There is the sacramental interpretation which teaches that it is the performance of baptism that incorporates us into Christ. That is the doctrine of baptismal regeneration, as taught by Roman Catholics, Anglo-Catholics and others. It is governed by their belief that grace is transmitted by and in the elements employed, whether they be the bread and wine of the Lord's Supper or the water of baptism.

Then there are those who say that what is taught by this passage is that the baptism referred to means our baptismal vows, by which we declare our faith, repudiate the life of sin and pledge ourselves to a new way of life. This, they claim, puts us into the realm and sphere of Christ. But it must be emphasised in this connection, that the significance of baptism does not rest in anything that the person being baptised may *do* or *say,* but rather in the fact that it is confirming and sealing *to* that person the great miracle of grace whereby he or she has been incorporated into Christ.

Some have interpreted this passage as meaning that we are baptised into the sphere of Christ's influence. But what is taught here is not only that we have come under the influence of Christ, or into the sphere of His influence, but that we are spiritually united to Christ. As we *were* "in Adam" so we *are* "in Christ".

Others interpret this passage as saying that baptism is a sign of our belief in the redeeming and saving efficacy of the death of Christ as a propitiation for our sins. "How shall we, that are dead to sin, live any longer therein?" But again it must be said that it is not merely a declaration that we *believe* this, but also that we are *actually united* to Christ. "We have been planted together — " this is union.

Another interpretation, which is that normally considered as the traditional Baptist interpretation, says that baptism is the symbolic representation, or pictorial enactment, of a deeper spiritual reality, namely, our union with Christ; our union with Him in His death and in His burial. We go down under the water — a picture of burial — and then come up again out of the water, which is a picture of resurrection.

In view of the importance of this matter, and particularly with regard to the place it occupies in connection with the whole subject before us, it is necessary for us to examine this passage a little more closely in order to determine whether or not this understanding, which is held to by the Baptists, is its correct interpretation.

First of all let us notice that Paul does not say that this is a *picture representing* something. He says "We *are* buried with Him *by* baptism. . ." or "through baptism".

As we have already noticed we have in this passage a reference to the great doctrine of our spiritual, mystical union with Christ. This doctrine tells us that we are united with Him in *all* that happened to Him. The first thing to be remembered is that we were crucified with Him. In Rom.6: 5 we are told that we have been planted together. Paul tells us in Eph.2: 6 that not only are we raised up together (with Christ) but we have been made to "sit together in heavenly places in Christ Jesus". Not *all* these things are represented by baptism. So this causes us to query the notion that baptism is a pictorial representation of our union with Christ; bearing in mind also that Paul makes no reference to baptism in his above mentioned statement in Eph.2.

Having rejected *that* interpretation, it must be replaced by what would seem to be a more Scripturally based interpretation, and when looked at in the way which we will now consider, it should have an appeal to all who genuinely seek the truth at all costs.

Let us start by noting the statement again. It is, we agree, referring to the union of believers with Christ. Now Paul says this union takes place through baptism. All believers have been "baptised into Jesus Christ". We must therefore enquire as to what sort of baptism Paul has in mind here, and it would seem that the answer is to be found in his first epistle to the Corinthians chapter 12 verse 13. "For by one Spirit are we all baptised into one body, whether we be Jews or Gentiles — ". It is a baptism *by* the Holy Spirit, not to be confused with the baptism *with* the Holy Spirit such as was manifest on the Day of Pentecost. It is by means of the gracious ministry of the Spirit that each individual believer is joined to the mystical body of Christ. That is the great theme of the Corinthian passage. How else does it happen if not by the Spirit? And this essential and vital work of the Spirit is called baptising *into* Christ, just as He, the Spirit, and He alone, brings about our regeneration. So we must inevitably conclude that Paul is *not* referring to water baptism in this passage. Nor is he referring to it in Gal.3: 27, nor in Eph.4: 5, in which places reference is again being made to the activity of the Holy Spirit in uniting the believer to the Lord Jesus Christ.

It seems to me that as we are brought to recognise the weaknesses in the Baptist interpretation of this passage, we can find wonderful satisfaction, that can only come with the dawning of some further aspect of divine truth, as we reflect on how perfectly the interpretation which I have just outlined fits the doctrine of our union with Christ. It is the doctrine which tells us that Christ is our federal Head and Representative, and it is only on account of this that Paul could be so bold as to say "God hath quickened us (by His Spirit — regeneration) together with Christ, . . . and hath raised us up together, and made us sit together in heavenly places in Christ Jesus" (Eph.2:4–6). We must be careful that we do not obliterate some of the glorious benefits that accrue to God's people, on account of our union with Christ, by mistaking some of the Scriptures which speak to us of this blessed truth. It is *because* we are united to Him that we derive all these benefits. It is *because* we are united to Him that our final salvation is guaranteed; for everything that happened to Him has happened to us. And it is the Spirit who unites us to Christ. That is the baptism about which the apostle is here speaking.

TEACHING OF COLOSSIANS CHAPTER 2

In conclusion a brief reference must be made to the passage in Paul's epistle to the Colossians (chapter 2, verses 11 & 12). I say *brief*, because the same sort of arguments apply here, as to the passage in Romans. Paul is again dealing with the subject of our union with Christ. This is the way William Hendriksen paraphrases these two verses, by way of exposition:—

"You, believers, have no need of external circumcision. You

have received a far better circumcision, that of heart and life. That circumcision is yours by virtue of your union with Christ. When He was buried you — that is, your former, wicked selves — were buried with Him. When He was raised you — as new creatures — were raised with Him.''

As we have observed elsewhere the rite of circumcision, as well as its other signification, represented union with Christ. So here in this passage, we have both the Old Testament and New Testament signs and seals of the Covenant brought together, each equally signifying to God's redeemed people their union with Christ, the significance of which is developed and enlarged upon here by Paul, and at the same time showing to us how circumcision has been substituted by baptism in the Christian era.

We must therefore conclude, in the light of the foregoing discussion, that the two chief grounds of the Baptist argument, namely that the word ''baptism'' invariably means immersion, and that such passages as Rom.6: 3–6 plainly teach immersion, are seen to be unsubstantial, and that the *mode* of baptism is therefore not of the *essence* of the symbolism. So long as water is used in the name of the Trinity, the precise mode of administering the ordinance is left an open question. Indeed, when we consider the variations in climate and temperature throughout the world; the variations of the geographical circumstances, influencing the availability of water; and the variations in the health of the person to be baptised; all these and other considerations tend to favour the mode of sprinkling on account of its universal suitability.

"I will take you from among the heathen, and gather you out of all countries, and will bring you into your own land. Then will I sprinkle clean water upon you, and ye shall be clean: from all your filthiness, and from all your idols, will I cleanse you. A new heart also will I give you, and a new spirit will I put within you, and cause you to walk in My statutes, and ye shall keep My judgments, and do them. And ye shall dwell in the land that I gave to your fathers; and ye shall be My people, and I will be your God."

Ezekiel 36: 24–28.

THE ARCHAEOLOGY OF THE MODE OF BAPTISM

Attention has been given by some, in connection with the mode of baptism, to the existence of evidence contained in antique *remains* and *monuments* relating to the first few centuries of the Christian Church. The argument put forward, by those who favour this approach, to a solution to the age-long dispute concerning the correct mode of Christian baptism, is this. The early Church, particularly during, and immediately following, the time of the apostles, must, it is thought, have practised the correct mode of baptism, and therefore, if evidence of this kind can be produced, to show what the generally accepted practice was, *that* would surely be the end of the argument.

It is intended, therefore, in this section, to investigate this approach to the subject and to see what records exist to provide the sort of evidence that is required. The whole subject of the archaeology of baptism is discussed by C. F. Rogers in "Studia Biblica et Ecclesiastica, Vol. V, Part 4: Oxford 1903". There may be some evidence in the *writings* of the early fathers, but also, and in particular, we will be giving consideration to any evidence which may have been discovered in the form of *archaeological remains,* such as vessels used in the administering of this sacrament, and pictorial representations of the rite being administered.

EVIDENCE OF ANCIENT WRITINGS

We will first consider the evidence of the *writings* of the early

Church fathers. As far as can be ascertained, the first three centuries of the Christian Church furnish no instance of any local church gathering, or writer of those times, opposing infant baptism on principle, on the grounds of considering it to be an unacceptable form of baptism. Nor, in that same early period of the Christian Church, has there been found a single instance recorded of an adult person being baptised when that person had been born to Christian parents. This is very important evidence in favour of the paedobaptist interpretation of the Biblical teaching on Christian baptism. It will be appreciated that the paedobaptist view embraces adult baptism (for those whose parents were *not* Christian) and infant baptism for those whose parents *were* Christian.

It would, of course, be a task of great patience and industry to produce evidence to support these statements. Indeed, the very nature of the statements renders it more appropriate to search the historical records for an instance which might *refute* them. The source of information is sufficiently reliable for the matter to be left open for denial should verifiable evidence to the contrary be discovered. However the assertion is made in good faith.

Baptism was, it would seem, frequently deferred until the approach of death, but this policy was based on the erroneous and superstitious idea that post-baptismal sins were much more serious than those committed before being baptised. This affords an example of the corruption that had already penetrated into the teaching of the Church even at this very early stage, and for this reason the evidence provided by the writings of the early fathers is very uncertain and unreliable.

In the fourth century it is a well known fact that a great doctrinal controversy raged concerning the sovereign purposes of God in His plan for the salvation of man. The principal proponents concerned were Pelagius and Augustine. But the interesting fact is that *both* these leading thinkers of the Church in those days, upheld infant baptism. Pelagius, who had travelled over most of the Christian world, said that he "had never heard of even any impious heretic who refused the ordinance to infants". Augustine expressed his own thoughts in a similar way.

Pursuing the matter of historical evidence a little further, some consideration might reasonably be given to the place of importance given to it by those who occupy the traditional Baptist viewpoint concerning the Biblical teaching on Christian baptism. Most Christians are agreed, whether Baptist or paedobaptist, that the rite of baptism is an essential part of the Christian teaching, associated with the Christian Church. The Baptist asserts that baptism by immersion is the *only* valid form of baptism according to the teaching of the Bible, and that infant baptism cannot be recognised as such.

In support of this assertion the Baptist claims that ''believer's baptism'' alone was the practise of the Church in the period immediately following the apostolic age. Baptists would acknowledge that there *have* been periods when infant baptism has been practised, but they would say that *that* was an error on the part of the Church. Now where disputes have occurred in the history of the Church, regarding important matters of doctrine and Church order, the Church has almost always left on record copious details of the words and writings of the disputants, but there is *no record of any such controversy,* which one would naturally expect to have found, if such a radical change had taken place in the Church's practice of the rite of baptism.

In this connection it must be acknowledged that Tertullian (third century) seems to have been the only exception, insofar as *he did* oppose infant baptism, but not on doctrinal grounds, but rather on grounds of expediency. This does not however carry with it any great significance, as his expressed views on several points of Scriptural doctrine seem to be very dubious and unorthodox. But even Tertullian did not deny that paedobaptism was, and had been, current practice.

Origen, another of the early fathers (third century) repeatedly attests, in his writings, the practice and necessity of paedobaptism, which he regarded as an observance handed down from the apostles. He lived little more than 100 years after the apostolic age. It is said of him that ''he was inferior to none of the fathers in talent and erudition''. But again, it must be said of *him* that his writings reveal certain deficiences and errors in the field of Christian doctrine.

Wm. Cunningham, in his ''Historical Theology'', remarks, concerning the sad and surprisingly rapid deterioration during the first two centuries of the Christian Church of its role as a faithful custodian of the truth, that "the symbolical character of the sacraments was soon more or less obscured or lost sight of, and some traces of the Popish principles of the 'opus operatum' . . . began to make their appearance, which, in the progress of ignorance and corruption of the peculiar doctrines of Christianity, were gradually more and more developed". The situation, as here described by Cunningham, tends to diminish one's regard for the value of the *writings* of the early fathers with regard to their possible contribution to a solution of any particular doctrinal issue.

This hurried review of the available evidence found in the *writings* of the early fathers of the Church, shows, amongst other things, the somewhat unreliable nature of information emanating from that quarter. Great credit is due, however, to the men that carried the banner of the Cross on, from the days of the apostles, and perhaps their weaknesses in the realm of recorded statements of doctrine, only go to bring out in the sharpest contrast the character of *their* writings and the *infallible* and authoritative writings of their predecessors, the inspired apostles.

This much however may be said, by way of conclusion, in this respect. The extent to which paedobaptism is known to have prevailed in the third century is difficult to reconcile with the traditional Baptist teaching concerning the *prevalence* of the practice of believer's baptism at this early period. There remains a puzzling uncertainty in our minds. What form of baptism *was* actually practised, in the first few centuries of the Christian Church, as the prevailing and generally accepted method?

Although the major point of dispute between Christians, regarding Christian baptism, relates to the validity or non-validity of infant baptism, the orthodox Baptist teaching narrows it down even more. *They* say that not only is adult baptism the only valid and recognisable form of baptism within the Christian Church, but also the baptism administered to those adults must be by total immersion. They do not recognise sprinkling, or pouring, as valid modes of baptism.

EVIDENCE OF ANCIENT REMAINS

We now move on from our glance at the *writings* of the early fathers, for decisive evidence regarding details of baptism practised in the first few centuries of the Church, to consider whether any significant and decisive evidence exists amongst the *remains* of those early days.

I propose, at this point, to take advantage of the research that has been carried out in this subject by Dr. B. B. Warfield, who was a professor of theology in the Theological Seminary of Princeton, New Jersey, from 1887 to 1921. The many references made by him to the writings of other authorities, bear testimony to his wide ranging research into, and study of, this subject. For this reason I will be making frequent reference to his writings, giving extended quotations of his actual words, so as to benefit from the conclusions and considerations and opinions which he has expressed, resulting from his extensive reading and research.

Concerning the evidence, in general, which is available from the *remains* of those early centuries, Warfield has the following to say:—

> ''The evidence of the practice of affusion, or pouring, as something more than an unusual and extraordinary mode of baptism, which fails us in the *writings* of the Fathers, seems to be provided, however, in the *monumental* representations of the rite. We read in one of the latest and most judicious handbooks of Christian archaeology: 'It is most noteworthy that from the second to the ninth century there is found scarcely one pictorial representation of baptism by immersion; but the suggestion is almost uniformly sprinkling or pouring'. (Bennett, ''Christian Archaeology'' 1890.)
>
> ''Representations which clearly indicate immersion, neither were impossible nor are altogether lacking; but they bear no proportion in number to those which seem to imply the act of pouring, or affusion, and when clear, are usually of *late* date. On the other hand, representations in which affusion seems to be implied, are of *all* ages, and comparatively numerous. The fact is so obvious, indeed, that with a bald statement of it we might be tempted to conclude that the literary and monumental evidences stand in hopeless contradiction.'' (B. B. Warfield, ''Studies in Theology. Vol.IX.'' p.361.)

REMAINS DEPICTING BAPTISM OF LORD JESUS CHRIST

When further referring to the *monumental* evidence available, in which we are at present particularly interested, Warfield speaks of there being a sharp distinction between *two series of representation* — those which depict the historical scene of the baptism of Christ, and those which depict ordinary baptism. Speaking of the influence that each of these series has upon the other he remarks:—

> ''Artists seeking to represent the rite of baptism have not always given a perfectly realistic rendering of the service as seen by them day after day in their own baptistery, but have allowed reminiscences of familiar representations of our Lord's baptism to affect their treatment. And on the other hand they have not been able to exclude the influence of the rite of baptism as customarily administered before their eyes, from affecting their representation of Christ's baptism''.

The obvious point under consideration here is the fact that the baptism of the Lord Jesus Christ was a most vitally important landmark in the historical background of God's great plan of redemption for sinful mankind. It was an outstanding event of the first order of importance and worthy of being the subject of monumental works of art. So the monumental records and remains of this event will undoubtedly display evidences of a dual role. They will give some hint as to the mode of baptism practised at that time, but being virtually impossible of being separated from the uniqueness of the Person depicted as being baptised, it takes on more the role of an historical monument marking an historical event of the greatest significance. Concluding his remarks on the series representing the baptism of Christ, Warfield says —

> ''It is hardly possible to understand the manner in which the artists have pictured to themselves the baptism of Christ, without postulating familiarity on their part with baptism as something else than a simple immersion''.

I have just referred to Warfield's convenient division of the various sorts of monumental evidence of the early practice of the rite of baptism, into that special group that depicts the baptism of Christ, and which understandably is the centre of particular interest, and that group which depicts the straightforward procedure which seems to have been followed in those early days when anyone, at any time, was the subject of this rite. It may have been thought that if it could be established what form of baptising John the Baptist used, when he baptised the Lord Jesus Christ, then this would have been the end of all dispute. However, as has been mentioned elsewhere in this treatise, we should bear in mind that the baptism with which the Lord Jesus Christ was baptised, was related to the ceremonial law, as was also His circumcision. Christ *Himself* being the originator and ordainer of Christian baptism. But quite apart from this fact, as has been seen, it must be admitted that the ancient representations of this rite, in the case of Christ's baptism, are by no means conclusive.

REMAINS DEPICTING GENERAL AND ORDINARY INCIDENTS OF BAPTISM

But to complete this present review, regard must be given to the second grouping of this monumental evidence, in other words, to the *general* and *ordinary* incidents of baptism which have been recorded in ancient *monuments* and *representations*. What do we find here? As they are uncomplicated by being associated with any person of renown, do they leave a clearer record or testimony?

The series of cases belonging to the former grouping, that is, the records relating to the baptism of Christ, started by considering a fresco in the crypt of Lucina in the Roman catacombs, seeming to belong to the opening of the second century. The *second* series, that of *general* cases of baptism in those early days, and which we are now going to consider, also begins in the Roman catacombs, in the so-called Sacramental Chapel of the catacombs of Callistus, and in particular in relation to two frescoes dating from the opening of the third century. I quote from Warfield here:—

> "In both of these (frescoes) the river is still presupposed — probably a trait in representing baptismal scenes borrowed from the typical instance of the baptism of Christ. Into it the neophyte (by this Warfield means a new convert. As in 1 Tim.3:6 "novice") has descended, but the water scarcely reaches his ankles. John stands on the adjoining ground with his right hand on the neophyte's head. In one of the pictures

> a cloud of water surrounds the head. In neither case is a complete immersion possible; and in one of them affusion seems to be evident."

Warfield then proceeds to refer to some remains associated with the period after the time of Constantine, which he describes as "three especially important monuments". One of these three monuments is "a gravestone from Aquileia on which the neophyte stands in a shallow font and water descends on him from above". The second of the three is "a silver spoon from Aquileia on which the water descends on the head of the neophyte from the beak of the dove", and the third is "a glass fragment found in the ruins of an old Roman house, representing a girl upon whom water descends from a vase, while she is surrounded with spray from it".

It will no doubt be appreciated that at this stage, the purpose in mentioning these various details is that the evidence which they may provide, in support of any particular interpretation of the Biblical teaching concerning Christian baptism, should be recorded and allowed to present its own evidence. Consequently, what is now being put before you rather amounts to a catalogue of examples, presented in a rather disconnected form.

Another example relates to a somewhat later period (c.827), and is a representation of the baptism of St. Ambrose on the famous Paliotto in S. Ambrogio at Milan. "Here the recipient stands in a font up to his middle and the priest pours water on his head from a vase". Warfield then adds "The later examples fall entirely in line with these earlier ones". He goes on to quote Kirsche as saying "A complete immersion is not found in the West even in the first period of the Middle Ages, but the form of representation which we have just noted (for Warfield used the same source of information for the examples just quoted) goes over into the later art with certain modifications". But he goes on, "We need not pause to note the examples — of what seems the general course of later art representations; our interest will naturally centre in the earlier examples already cited. In them seems to be borne an unbroken testimony of baptism by affusion".

Warfield discusses fairly fully a debate that has arisen between the seemingly opposing meanings arising from a study of *monumental* evidence, on the one hand, and *literary* evidence on the other. Efforts have been made by various experts in this field to reconcile the apparent differences. The literary evidence seeming to represent immersion, and the monumental evidence representing affusion.

Warfield writes:— "The only theory known to us which seems to do full justice to both classes of facts — those gathered from the literature and monuments alike — is that which De Rossi has revived and given the support of his great name. This supposes that normal baptism was performed in the early Church by a mode which united immersion and affusion in a single rite — not as in the Armenian rite, making them separate parts of a repeated ritual". (De Rossi still insists that the performance of the rite by pouring was by no means exceptional in the early Church).

Drawing a few of these opinions and findings together, Warfield says, indicating his intention to scrutinise the two lines of evidence somewhat sharply — "We will observe, for example, that though affusion is emphasised by the monuments, it is not necessarily a *simple* affusion. The candidate stands in water, which reaches to his ankles or even to his knees in the earlier pictures, and in the later ones to his waist or above. Hence Dr. Schaff says 'Pouring on the head while the candidate stands on dry ground, receives no aid from the catacombs'. This is a rather extreme statement. The fresco in the catacomb of Praetextatus, if it be thought to represent baptism, would be a very early example to the contrary (namely, of the candidate standing on dry ground)*; and symbolical representations on somewhat later monuments . . . do not indicate water below". The conclusion that some seem to have come to is that the important aspect of the rite is the application of water to the head. And this was achieved either by pouring water from a vessel onto the head, or by immersing the head. Referring to this Warfield says, "The extant fonts also suggest this form of the rite. And the *literary* notices themselves are filled with indications that the mode of baptism thus suggested was the common mode throughout the Christian world".

"We may then probably assume", he says, "that normal patristic baptism was by a trine immersion upon a standing catechumen, and that this immersion was completed either by

*Author's parenthesis.

lowering the candidate's head beneath the water, or (possibly more commonly) by raising the water over his head and pouring it upon it''.

''For Tertullian'', Warfield says, ''the analogies of baptism were to be found in the Jewish lustrations and the heathen rites of cleansing; and so fundamental is this conception of baptism to him, that it takes precedence of every other; though these rites were performed by sprinkling they yet remain rites of the same class with baptism''.

Referring to these various early evidences of the rite of Christian baptism, Warfield gives a cautionary note that we must be careful, even though they *are* very early monuments, and evidences, not to assume that there have *not* been significant changes taking place in the realm of Church procedures, even by the time of the *second* century. Indeed he said that by the middle of the second century there *were* changes to be seen: ''The bishop, for example, was already a different officer from what he was in the days when the New Testament was written; and the Epistle of Clement of Rome witnesses to quite another church system from that which was in operation in the days of Irenaeus. . . . The *second* century, in a word, marks a considerable advance on the *first* in the development of church usages; and it is necessary to exercise great caution in assuming what we find to be the practice of this century to be also apostolic, merely because it represents the earliest usage which we can trace''.

PROSELYTE — BAPTISM

We turn now to enquire concerning the relation of Christian baptism to what is known as proselyte-baptism, or the rabbinical custom of initiating proselytes into the Jewish faith by a formal and complete ablution. This is a matter of the greatest interest in connection with the subject before us. If we pause to ask ourselves ''What *is* Christian baptism?'' we must surely be faced with the matter of *the time and manner of its introduction*. For instance, when John called on the people to come to *his* baptism we do not imagine that the rite which John was administering was a complete novelty. On the contrary, it appears that John expected to be thoroughly understood at the outset, it being an old and very well understood rite. This then, the rabbinical custom of initiating Jewish proselytes, might appear to have been the pattern on which the rite of Christian baptism was based. With this in mind, were it possible to find out details of the *former* rite, it would seem to be reasonable to expect to discover, in these details, some outlines at least of the way in which *Christian baptism* was administered at the establishment of the Christian Church.

In this connection we may again turn to B. B. Warfield's writings which provide a considerable amount of valuable information. It seems that literature on this subject is copious, a guide to which is found in Schürer's "Jewish People in the time of Jesus Christ", para. 31, note 302. Schürer says that no one has influenced modern opinion on the subject so much as Schneckenburgher.

Elsewhere in this treatise emphasis has been placed on the similarity between the rite of circumcision in the Old Testament economy and the rite of baptism in the New Testament economy. Both, in their respective eras, being the divinely appointed signs and seals of the Covenant of Grace. It is important to bear this in mind as we consider this ancient Jewish rite of proselyte-baptism. This rite had an entirely different significance from that associated with New Testament Christian baptism. Christian baptism is a seal of the Covenant, but this Jewish baptism was not a seal of the Covenant, but was a part of, or derived from, the Jewish ceremonial washings, some reference to which being found in Heb. 9:10:— "meats and drinks, and divers washings —".

Warfield says:— "It is scarcely possible to overstate the importance which the rabbis attached to baptism, in the reception of proselytes. It was held to be absolutely necessary to the making of a proselyte".

This point brought out by Warfield, is something which we should not pass by without the most serious reflection. It may here be observed that the Jewish religious leaders had introduced, amongst their many additional "carnal ordinances" (Heb. 9:10) (which the Lord Jesus Christ is referring to in Matt.5:20 when He speaks of "the righteousness of the scribes and Pharisees"), the initiating rite of proselyte-baptism. And this, as we have seen, served as an acceptance certificate for a person wishing to be received as a fully accredited Jew. Here there is a clear, and intended, connection between the act of being baptised, and the actual acceptance of such a person as a "bona fide" member of God's chosen race. This is of considerable interest when taken into the context of Christian baptism, and the acceptance of an individual into membership of the company of God's chosen people, who have been redeemed by the Lord Jesus Christ. It might well be that *this* was the original "back door", reflected in so-called "baptismal regeneration", by which many have mistakenly thought that access has been obtained into Christ's Kingdom.

On this matter of the great importance of baptism in the minds of the Jewish leaders, Warfield goes on to show how there was not *complete* uniformity of opinion amongst them. He says, "Rabbi Eliezer maintained that circumcision without baptism sufficed, Rabbi Joshua on the other hand contended that baptism without circumcision was enough, while the scribes contended that both rites were necessary".

The following quotation is from a work by Edersheim entitled "The Life and Times of Jesus the Messiah". — This constitutes a description of the procedure for a person purposing to become a Jew. The whole procedure is threefold, comprising circumcision, baptism and a sacrifice. However I quote from the description of the *baptismal* ceremony only — "The proselyte, in the presence of the three teachers (who had also witnessed his circumcision and who now served as witnesses of the baptism, under the name of "*fathers* of the baptised", corresponding to the nature of the baptism as a "new birth") cut his hair and nails, undressed completely, and entered the water until his arms were covered. The Commandments were now read to him, and, solemnly engaging to obey them, he perfected the baptism by completely immersing himself".

However, as Warfield remarks, "the discovery of connection between the two rites (i.e. Jewish and Christian baptism) is no immediate proof that *one* owes its existence to the *other*". If any case is to be made out for Christian baptism, and the actual procedures associated with it, being structured on the procedures for Jewish baptism, then it becomes a matter of great moment to determine whether the Jewish ceremony existed when Christian baptism was instituted. If it *did* exist at that time, it would be very understandable that there would be a similarity between the two, in the absence of any word to the contrary to be found in the New Testament. And it must be borne in mind in this connection, that the earthly ministry of the Lord Jesus Christ extended over this ''transition period'', a time when His disciples, as well as John the Baptist, were baptising people.

When it is remembered that the orthodox Jew did not recognise the coming of the Lord Jesus Christ as the Messiah, it is reasonable to visualise that His coming was no interruption of the performing of the various Jewish ceremonial rituals. Having in mind particularly their many washings, it is conceivable that they continued for quite a long period concurrently with Christian baptism. Warfield writes — ''direct testimony to the existence of proselyte-baptism fails us in the midst of the second century after Christ, but nevertheless something of the nature of a cleansing bath must be presupposed from the very beginning, as a part of the reception of the proselyte. Delitzsch calls attention to a point which appears to be of importance for understanding the *origin* of the rite, when he adverts to the connection of this bath with the sacrifice, so that its prescription must date from a time previous to the cessation of the sacrifices.'' At this point Warfield quotes Delitzsch:— ''Its origin (namely, the origin of the rite of proselyte-baptism)* also in itself presupposes the existence of the Temple, and the cleansings required by its sacrificial services, which were performed by plunge-baths. ... Beyond doubt cleansing by means of a plunge-bath was already, from a very early time, demanded of the heathen, after he had been circumcised, as a pre-condition of his participation in the sacrificial services''.

It is interesting to notice that the original rite of washing seems to have been linked to the offering of sacrifices. But when the Temple was destroyed, and the sacrifices consequently ceased, the washing rite continued. But in that event, it appears that the proselytes were still required to *promise to sacrifice* when the Temple was restored.

It can be seen from the foregoing that although we may see certain similarities, when comparing this somewhat elaborate Jewish ritual of proselyte-baptism with Christian baptism, they are in fact two distinct and different rites, although their forms

*Author's parenthesis.

may perhaps have a common origin in the cleansing lustrations of the Jewish law, as we find them in the Scriptures.

Delitzsch says "The baptism of John and proselyte-baptism stand only in indirect relation to one another, insofar as one and the same idea underlies both kinds of baptism, as well as the legal lustrations in general". It is a matter of great importance which Delitzsch proceeds to emphasise when he says "There is no reason to assume that ... Christian baptism originated in proselyte-baptism, or even that it derived only its *form* from it. It was, moreover, unlike the economy of God, to build upon a *Pharisaic usage* and not rather upon an *ancient symbol,* already sanctified by the giving of the Law on Sinai. John himself assigns the choice of this symbolical rite (namely, the baptism that he administered)* to divine appointment ("He ... sent me to baptise with water" Jn.1: 33) ... However, in conformity with the nature of the New Covenant as a fulfillment of 'the law' and 'the prophets' (Matt.5: 17), over and above its connection with the ceremonial Law, and the Levitical lustrations in general as prescribed in it, Christian baptism has also *another* point of connection, in *prophecy,* in the prediction of a future purification and sanctification through water and the Spirit (Ezek. 36: 25; 37: 23f; Is.44: 3; Zech. 13: 1)".

CONCLUSION

So we return to the matter raised at the beginning of this present consideration, when we set out to discover whether, at the time of John the Baptist or at the commencement of the Christian era, the rite of baptism was quite a *novel* thing, or whether people were *then* very familiar with its general idea.

We must come to the conclusion, in the light of the foregoing considerations, that (to quote Warfield) "Christian baptism was not such a new thing that it could not be understood by the disciples to whom it was committed. It had its very close connection with precedent and well-known rites. But its connection was not specifically with proselyte-baptism as subsequently developed into a formal rite of initiation into Judaism." Warfield then concludes that Christian baptism was not directly

*Author's parenthesis.

connected with proselyte-baptism, but with the prophetical predictions of Messianic cleansing, and the cleansing lustrations of the Old Testament Law; both baptisms seeming to spring from the same origins.

It has become apparent that this so-called proselyte-baptism is something which developed from its simpler earlier forms, which existed at the close of the Old Testament era, into a somewhat complex threefold initiatory rite. And indeed this complex form seemed to develop during the second century. Consequently, in the words of Warfield, "We are left without ground from this quarter for any stringent inferences as to the mode of the first administration of Christian baptism. The idea of lustrations was bathing for the sake of cleansing; and the 'many baptisms' of the Jews were performed in more modes of application of the water than one. The prophetic announcements in like manner run through all possible modes of applying the water. In *any* mode of application it was *complete cleansing* which was *symbolised*. Beyond that, it would seem, we cannot proceed on this pathway".

Well, we have pursued various lines of investigation which might have seemed to hold out prospects of success in determining what procedures were actually followed in the period of the Church's life immediately following the times of the apostles. We have considered some of the available records of monuments such as fonts and baptisteries and pictorial representations of the baptismal rite being administered. We have also considered the writings of those who have made a special study of this subject, and particularly paying attention to the possible significance of the Jewish proselyte-baptisms currently being practised in the first or second centuries, and the possibility of any direct relationship between that Jewish baptismal rite and Christian baptism. We have come to see that there are no grounds for concluding that there was any direct relationship between these two baptisms, but that most likely they both sprang from the same origins.

Warfield suggests, on the basis of the investigations mentioned, that by scrutinising and analysing the available recorded information it is not possible to arrive at any finality in this matter of endeavouring to determine the true mode to be employed when administering Christian baptism. Someone might be inclined to question the wisdom of pursuing these lines at all, especially when they fail to produce any positive and definitive results.

However, it seems to me that in this general study of the subject of Christian baptism, we are under some obligation to give consideration to these representations, monuments and records of ancient practices, in order to discover whether or not they contained clear evidences with regard to the *mode* of Christian baptism. Someone who has read this treatise, and followed its reasoning so far, and who still retained doubts as to the true mode and practice of Christian baptism, might have been of the opinion that the matter *could* have been resolved by resort to a study of these ancient records, thinking that *this* would prove to be ''an end of all strife'' (Heb.6: 16). Should such an opinion have been held by anyone, it is hoped that the foregoing investigation will serve to prove, at least, that certainty regarding details of the mode of Christian baptism *cannot* be obtained by this means.

How then may it be determined? All candid, thinking, Christians are desirous of resolving this difficulty. It would seem to be very fitting and humbling to discover again that we are ultimately shut up to the teaching contained in God's holy and infallible Word. God knows His purpose in these things, and He has recorded and revealed all that He requires of His redeemed people *there.* Some might be inclined to enquire why these things have not been made clearer, so that disputes amongst God's people, concerning His requirements, would not have arisen. It would seem that God has seen to it that there ''are some things hard to be understood'' (2 Pet.3:16) in order that we may be kept humble. The truth is not always on the surface, but may be hidden in the *deep mines* of God's Word, demanding of us the *greatest industry* in digging deep into these inexhaustible mines of His revelation. It is for this reason that considerable space has been *given* in this treatise, to the study and interpretation of the Biblical teaching concerning Christian baptism.

"It came to pass, that, while they communed together and reasoned, Jesus Himself drew near, and went with them."

Luke 24:15.

THE REFORMED BAPTIST POSITION

So far I have made scarcely any reference to, or acknowledgment of, the interpretation of Scriptural teaching relating to Christian baptism as understood by our friends who occupy the Baptist position, and who hold their generally accepted understanding of this subject. I now propose to redress that imbalance somewhat by taking note of their case as presented by one of their proponents.

I have chosen for particular examination a book, which was first published in its complete form in 1973 under the title ''Children of Abraham'', the author being Rev. David Kingdon, then the Principal of the Irish Baptist College. By some Reformed adherents to the Baptist position it has been heralded as the most significant book on baptism to have been written in this century from the Calvinistic Baptist point of view.

It should, I think, be stated at this point, in case any might take exception to any views which will be referred to, that Mr. Kingdon does not claim to be speaking on behalf of *all* Baptists. In his Introduction he acknowledges the fact that the majority of adherents to the world-wide Baptist movement occupy a position which could be described, for want of a better term, as non-Calvinistic. Those in this position generally do not (so I believe) recognise the principle of federal theology. The difference between *their* position and the one which I am propounding in this treatise, is rather more radical than the difference between Mr. Kingdon's interpretation and mine. It is, I believe, for this very reason, necessary to isolate the points of difference which seemingly exist between our two positions, which in other respects hold to the traditionally Reformed interpretations.

AREAS OF AGREEMENT

There are certain aspects of this book, as already intimated, which I find particularly gratifying, in so far as acknowledgment is given of certain basic principles and truths which are embodied in the pages of this treatise, and which seem to be so important to the establishing of a proper background to an understanding of the subject before us. I think that it would be advantageous therefore to bring out at this stage, the points of agreement, so that the points of disagreement may be more readily identified for later examination.

First of all, Mr. Kingdon acknowledges the importance of recognising the principle of federal theology, springing out of God's free and sovereign grace. This is a subject which I have already dealt with fairly fully and it is therefore sufficient now to make note of the fact that Mr. Kingdon sees this to be an undeniable principle operating in all of God's dealings with mankind, and in particular in His dealings with His own people, in terms of the Covenant of Grace.

There is no ambiguity with regard to his understanding of the Covenant of Grace, as he illustrates it by quoting fully from Prof. J. Murray's book entitled "Christian Baptism". He brings out by means of this quotation, the following points:

1) God deals with His elect people, whom He purposes to redeem, on the basis of a Covenant: that is, in His sovereign grace He binds Himself to save His Church. God's Covenant demands, that go with the revelation of Covenant grace, are summed up in these words: "Walk before Me, and be thou perfect" (Gen.17:1). The manifestation of grace calls forth the loving obedience of those who enjoy the blessings of the Covenant, which same principle can be recognised in Rom.12:1.

2) The infant seed of believing parents are embraced together with their parents, in the Covenant relation and provisions. In other words the blessings of the Covenant are promised, not to believing adults only, but to their children also, *who do not yet believe,* yet who are none the less included within the Covenant along with their parents (Gen.17: 7–10).

I am not suggesting that Kingdon agrees with all the implications which flow from this principle of federal theology but that he recognises the principle itself.

Kingdon's observations on certain general views held by some Baptists, which views he does not share, are quite helpful in that they indicate the possible alternative views held by them. Referring to the foregoing observations on the principle of covenant theology, Kingdon remarks: "The reaction of many present-day Baptists to the type of reasoning expoounded here, is to dismiss it very simply as 'Old Testament teaching'. When confronted by the analogy between circumcision and baptism they deny that there is any connection whatsoever between the two ordinances; the one they say is Old Testament, the other New Testament. Yet they do not dismiss the analogy between the Passover and the Lord's Supper in the same way. . . . But if one writes off the Old Testament in such a fashion what then becomes of the unity of the Bible?"

Kingdon mentions the names of some Particular (Calvinistic) Baptists who acknowledge the principle of federal theology, which the Scriptures show to be the basis of God's dealings with men, citing Thomas Patient, John Bunyan, John Gill, Abraham Booth, Alexander Carson and C. H. Spurgeon.

Another area of common ground which I share with David Kingdon, is the acknowledgement of the principle of the unity of the Bible and of its revelation of God's uniform, single, continuing, purpose of salvation, from start to finish. Quoting Kingdon again: "The second reason why the argument for infant baptism based on covenant theology, continues to make such a strong appeal, is because it takes seriously the unity of the Bible. Its starting point is that there is one Covenant of Grace which has been operative in human history since the Fall . . . From the first disclosure of grace (Gen.3:15) to the final vision of John (Rev.21:2, 3). Holy Scripture shows that there is but one Covenant of Grace throughout all ages. From this unity of the Covenant certain conclusions follow:

a) There is one Church of God, purchased with the blood of Christ, which embraces the people of God in all ages, and in all places.

b) There is one way of salvation, namely repentance toward God and faith in our Lord Jesus Christ, the Mediator of the eternal Covenant.''

Although this is a statement made by David Kingdon for the purpose of defining the Covenant of Grace, as understood by Reformed theologians, it is clear that he is in agreement with it, with the following qualification (quoting) ''the Covenant of Grace, although it exhibits diversity of administrations in the time of promise and in the time of fulfilment, is none-the-less one Covenant''.

I have recorded this very fundamental common ground rather fully in order that we may the more readily identify the aspects of interpretation about which it appears that we are *not* agreed, to which we will now turn.

AREAS OF DISAGREEMENT IDENTIFIED

The method of procedure which I propose to adopt is this. I will first of all identify the points of interpretation concerning which we are not in agreement, without, in the first instance, offering any alternative understanding. Having brought to light the areas of disagreement I will then offer my alternative interpretation. Finally I will highlight the points of disagreement as these have emerged in the discussion.

Although Kingdon recognises the analogy that exists between circumcision and baptism, he is not prepared to leave it at that, but suggests that we must take notice of the nature of the analogy. He says that it can be seen from Gen.17 that the Covenant with Abraham had both dispensational and trans-dispensational elements. By which I understand him to mean that the Covenant confirmed to Abraham, had elements which related to the dispensation associated with Abraham, and it also had elements which were related to a period, or periods, which were beyond the borders of that dispensation. Or as Kingdon explains it ''the promised blessings of the Covenant were implemented, either in the period before the advent of Christ, or in the period after the advent, or in both.'' He is distinguishing here between Abraham's natural descendants and his spiritual descendants. Again, referring to the Old Testament dispensation he refers to God's promise of Canaan to Abraham.

Kingdon asks a pertinent question:— "Did not cicumcision have a national reference as a mark of national separation to God; marking off Jews as a race from the nations round about?" He goes on to warn that we must not say "that circumcision had a spiritual significance and is the sign of the Covenant of Grace" without at the same time recognising its national significance.

He maintains that "the Covenant made with Abraham . . . has both a temporal and an eternal aspect, an earthly and a heavenly substance." Referring to the earthly element, the promise of Canaan, he points out that this is not the inheritance of Christians.

Reference is made to the New Testament interpretation of circumcision in which its spiritual aspect is emphasised. In this connection it is claimed that circumcision in the Old Testament is a type of which inward circumcision (regeneration) is the antitype. He says "I would argue that the principle of believers and their seed no longer has covenantal significance, precisely because the age of fulfilment has arrived".

In Chapter 3 of his book Kingdon asserts that it is wrong to identify New Testament fulfilment of the Covenant promises in Christ with the Old Testament types. He says that we read the Old Testament into the New Testament. "In the Old Testament, participation in the temporal earthly blessings of the Covenant was sufficient to give a right to circumcision." He also states that those who hold to the interpretation of the Biblical teaching on baptism represented by this treatise, are embarrassed "by the circumcision of Abraham's servants. Should servants to-day be baptised if they work in Christian households?"

Having given a quotation from Calvin (in his Institutes) regarding the Old Testament teaching on circumcising infants, he asks "But have our children, we must ask, an hereditary right to salvation?"

In Chapter 4 of his book Kingdon sets himself the task of providing "an interpretation of believers' baptism which does justice to the truly Biblical insights of covenant theology". In his subsequent discussion he states "We heartily repudiate the charge our Reformed paedobaptist brethren frequently bring against us, namely, that in insisting upon the necessity of repentance and faith as the conditions on which we baptise, we are guilty of subjectivism, of emphasising human decision to the neglect of prevenient grace''.

Kingdon recognises that a Baptist theology of the Covenant must include a satisfactory definition of the relationship between the children of their church members and the Covenant. This subject, although touched on in Ch.4 is the main consideration of Chapters 5 & 6. Here he refers to the Passover/Lord's Supper analogy and asks ''Why do our Reformed paedobaptist friends deny the Lord's Supper to infants?'' Arguing of course from the paedobaptist view of infant baptism and the Lord's Supper.

Kingdon writes ''membership of natural Israel was conditional upon natural birth, whereas membership of the new covenant people is dependent upon re-birth''. He goes on ''Both the concept of the remnant, and the promise of the new covenant, mark the transference of religion from a nationalistic to an ecclesiastical basis''.

Kingdon argues that the baptism administered by John the Baptist demonstrates ''that membership of the nation by virtue of natural birth'' was not regarded by him ''as determinative for membership in the Messianic community''.

In Chapter 6 he uses Paul's teaching in Rom.9: 6ff. to prove that children of believing parents are not necessarily Christian. He indicates that this is contrary to the paedobaptist understanding.

He then gives consideration to the teaching on the subject of infant baptism which can be derived from the Gospel narratives relating to the Lord Jesus Christ and His dealings with little children.

Referring to 1 Cor.7:16 Kingdon writes that this ''does allow us to state that ... the children who are born are in a state of privilege'' ... but that this ''does not furnish a proper ground for baptism''.

FIRST PRINCIPLES

As there is a danger that truth may become obscured by a profusion of associated details, so that attention is diverted from the salient issues to secondary and associated matters, I will at this stage, before responding to any particulars related above, go back to the *first principles.* It will then, I hope, be appropriate to put those foregoing particulars into the context of the salient issues.

I have spent some considerable time already in this treatise, discussing the origin and character of the Covenant of Grace, and the intimate and vital relationship between it and the Church, and happily Kingdon and I are in agreement on these issues. I only stress at this point the need to keep these realities ever before our mind's eye when we come to consider the relationship of other matters to them. We must not imagine that the Church principle began with Abraham. No one who is concerned to come to an understanding of God's revelation could afford to overlook the fact of Abraham. He stands out as probably the most significant person of all time, apart from the Lord Jesus Christ Himself. But we must not allow *that* to cloud our view of the overall strategy of God — from eternity to eternity.

After the entrance of sin into the world God founded His Church in the promise of the Messiah (Gen.3:15). That was a general promise to mankind, absolutely considered, proceeding from mere grace and mercy. Yet, as it was the foundation of the Church it included in it the nature of a covenant — the Covenant of Grace.

We must ask ourselves, with whom did God make this Covenant? Was it with every human being? or was it with some specific people? As we understand the teaching of the Bible, and this as we know is Reformed theology, God's Covenant of Grace was made with some specific people, and *not* with *all* people. Then we must ask ourselves who are these people? and in answering that question why should we try to choose a better term than the one which we find in the Bible, namely "the elect of God". The people given by the Father to the Son for the express purpose of redeeming them, giving them eternal life, keeping them, and raising them up at the last day (John 6: 39; 17: 2). In other words, the Church (See also Ps.50:5). What *condition* has God annexed to this Covenant by which a person is brought within its terms? The condition is *faith.* And how does God know that the elect of God will be able to exercise this vital appropriating grace of faith? The elect of God will be *given* this grace by God.

As soon as we define the beneficiaries of the Covenant as the elect of God, it is immediately clear that there is no other qualification but faith required by a person for him or her to be included within the terms of the Covenant. Indeed we can follow the line from Adam to Seth to Noah to Shem to Abraham. But the line does not stop there. It goes on to Paul to Athanasius to Luther and so on.

Another truth that becomes clear from this, is that the condition for participation in the Covenant has *always been* faith, and it *still is* faith. Paul says "thou standest by faith" (Rom.11: 20). In this connection it is important to remember that Abraham had this essential grace of faith before he received the sign and seal of circumcision (Rom.4:11).

I have deliberately emphasised this essentially spiritual character of the Covenant of Grace, and its associated promises, because of the tendency for the *minor* temporary, carnal, national, blessings, promised by God to Abraham, to blurr the *major* spiritual blessings promised, and associated with the Covenant of Grace. No one has, or ever had, or ever will have, any spiritual right to, or interest in, any of those promises or privileges, whatever his outward condition may be, but only by virtue of his incorporation in the Church, built on the Mediator of the new Covenant.

Before leaving the subject of the Covenant, we must bear in mind one matter, which I have dealt with in the section devoted to this subject. My concern at the moment is that we hold fast to the principle that God's everlasting mercies are revealed in, and related to, His everlasting Covenant; the Covenant of Grace. The Covenant of Works was that agreement between God and Adam, under the terms of which Adam fell. *That* Covenant was thereupon annulled, and there has never been another covenant of works. The Sinaitic Covenant was not a revised covenant of works, it was an appendix to the Covenant of Grace. I am stressing this point because some of the references to covenants in the epistle to the Hebrews might lead one to think that the Covenant of Grace was superseded by a "new covenant" (Heb.8: 13). The two covenants are two dispensations of the same basic unchangeable, spiritual, Covenant of Grace.

The prophecy of Jeremiah (Ch.31: 31—34) quoted by the Apostle in Heb.Ch.8: 8–12 makes the same distinction between "the covenant that I made with their fathers" and a "new" or "better" covenant. The very division of the Bible into the Old Testament and New Testament corresponds with these two "covenants" or administrations.

John Owen describes the two testaments as "That made with the church of Israel at Mount Sinai, and that made with us in the Gospel; not as absolutely as the Covenant of Grace, but as actually established in the death of Christ." Owen says also — "The new covenant, not a new covenant absolutely and originally, as given in the first promise, is intended; but in its complete Gospel administration, when it was actually established by the death of Christ . . . This, together with the covenant of Sinai, were, as most say, but different administrations of the same Covenant".

Another focal point, upon which we should concentrate our attention, is the fascinating and crucial teaching that we find in the Scriptures concerning the *seed* of Abraham. God chose Abraham out of the nations, giving to him not only a personal place in the Covenant, but also a *special* interest in it, by granting to him two privileges. *Firstly,* to be the progenitor of the Messiah according to the flesh, this privilege being a temporary one, having a limited season, and *secondly,* to be the pattern of the faith of the Church of all ages — past, present and future. Answerable to this twofold end of the separation of Abraham, there was a twofold seed allotted to him — a seed according to the flesh, and a seed according to the promise.

HISTORICAL MAP

Let us endeavour to visualise an historical map of the world. At the right extreme edge of the map is the beginning of time, and at the left extreme edge is the end of time.

Let us visualise a line running from the right hand edge towards the left, representing those people included within the terms of the Covenant. Or to be more specific, the elect of God. At a point along this line, say about one third of the way across the map from the start, Abraham appears. Then the line continues right across the map to the left hand edge. Somewhere in the centre of the map another Person appears; Jesus Christ. Now, on this map, draw another line from Abraham to Christ, which will represent Abraham's natural seed. At Abraham the line branches out as a family tree into a countless number of progeny; and just *one* of the branches leads to Christ. Now turning our attention to this Person, Jesus Christ. He also has a countless progeny — a spiritual progeny. From Christ we must draw on our map, lines to represent *His* family tree, the tree of His Church, which will be essentially different from Abraham's. From Christ myriads of lines proceed, and these, as well as going forward along the time scale, also go backwards. One terminating at Abraham himself, showing how he is vitally and spiritually related to the Head of the new humanity; the Head of the Church. A similar line links Christ with every individual believer, past and present; and other lines go on to the extreme left hand edge of the map.

NATURAL AND SPIRITUAL SEED OF ABRAHAM

This idea of an historical map may perhaps help to elucidate the situation, and hopefully it may help to bring out the relationship between the natural seed of Abraham and his spiritual seed; in so far as he was the pattern of the faith of the Church of all ages.

God's ancient promise to Abraham, confirmed and underlined by Paul, is the predominent factor in this whole area of consideration. ''Now to Abraham and his seed were the promises made. He saith not, And to seeds, as of many; but as of one, And to thy seed, which is Christ'' (Gal.3:16). As we know, God determined that Christ, according to the flesh, should come from the natural line of Abraham. ''Of whom as concerning the flesh Christ came'' (Rom.9:5).

The *major* theme, is that in the fulness of time Christ was to spring from Abraham's seed, according to the flesh. It was for this purpose that his posterity were separated from the rest of the world, and preserved as a peculiar people. The *minor* theme, and an inevitable corollary, is the development of the natural progeny of Abraham. As already mentioned, this was a temporary phase.

But, as so much in the Scriptures bears evidence, God often performs several things at the same time. An example of what I mean is this. When God brought the children of Israel into the land of Canaan, He was taking them into the land which He had promised to them, through Abraham. But this meant that the Canaanites had to go. What account had been taken of the rights of the Canaanites to stay in their land? God was doing two things. He was punishing the Canaanites for their great wickedness, and He was also keeping His promise to Abraham.

In addition to this, God was providing, by means of all the happenings of His chosen people, "figures of the true" (Heb.9:24). "All these things happened unto them for ensamples: and they are written for our admonition" (1 Cor.10:11). Their slavery in Egypt under the bondage of Pharaoh, their miraculous deliverance across the Red Sea, their pilgrimage through the wilderness, and all God's provisions for them, and His great patience with them. The miraculous crossing of the Jordan. The tabernacle and temple worship. All these were figurative of the heavenly realities, and perhaps nothing more so than the land of Canaan itself.

It is most significant that almost the entire nation, as it was when it came out of Egypt, was debarred by God, as an act of judgment, from entering into Canaan, because they did not have *faith,* as Abraham had (see Heb.3:18, also Heb.8:9). "I sware in My wrath that they should not enter into My rest" (Ps.95:11). The "rest" of Canaan was a figure of the spiritual rest of salvation into which God's people enter by faith *now,* in *this* world ("We which have believed do enter into rest" – Heb.4:3), which leads on to their ultimate, eternal, rest in heaven itself. The epistle to the Hebrews is full of teaching regarding the significance of the various episodes in the experiences of the children of Israel (e.g. chapters 3 & 4).

Whereas I have been emphasising the figurative aspect, and spiritual significance, of the history of the children of Abraham, we must not lose sight of the fact that they are nevertheless still a separate race of people, retaining their identity up to this very time in which we are living. But it is no part of the present study to consider what the Scriptures have to say about that nation in the future. The *greatest possible significance* attaches to the coming into this world of time of the promised Seed, and all matters of soteriological significance spring from Him, and from *that* point in history.

FIRST AND SECOND COVENANTS

The "first covenant" related to that dispensation to which the

Aaronical priesthood belonged. It was clearly intended by God, in His condescension to poor sinners, to display in considerable detail, by means of the shadowy types of the ceremonial law, and its sacrificial and temporary provision for the sins of His ancient people ("This is the blood of the testament which God hath enjoined unto you. ... And almost all things are by the law purged with blood; and without shedding of blood is no remission" — Heb.9:20, 22), the radical and all pervading nature of sin, and His threatened punishment on account of that sin, and the spiritual antitypes of His eternal provision for the condemning nature of sin, and of His promised heavenly and eternal blessings. No one, I suppose, would wish to dispute the fact of the typical character of this dispensation, this "first covenant." It is because it had this typical character that it would ultimately be eclipsed and overtaken and *abolished,* by that which it typified.

The "second covenant" relates to that dispensation which was introduced by the Lord Jesus Christ, of which He is the Mediator. The teaching of the epistle to the Hebrews is largely devoted to this very theme. The burden of its message is to establish the pre-eminence of Christianity above Judaism. It shows the great superiority of Jesus Christ, as the sum and substance of Christianity, as well as its Author, to all the great objects of Jewish veneration, including the Aaronical high priesthood. In the course of this argument, and inevitably, the great superiority is displayed of the second covenant over the first. Under the second covenant, Christ is displayed as the One who has abolished the Law as a rule of justification (which the Mosaic Law was typically, under the first covenant) by fulfilling the true, antitypical, Law of God, on behalf of the beneficiaries of the Covenant of Grace.

Many things associated with the first covenant can be recognised as typifying spiritual and eternal realities, the fulfilment of all of which can only be realised in the spiritual realm. In this respect, and in order to keep our thinking clear, we must be careful to notice the difference between something that God has appointed as a *sign,* and something that He has appointed as a *type.* The former has a very special function in the economy of God. By a *sign,* God obliges Himself to us, by, in this way, confirming His Covenant of Grace. Abraham received the sign of circumcision, a seal of the righteousness that came through faith

(Rom.4:11). It is something solidly tied to the Covenant of Grace. But a *type* represents a spiritual antitype. It therefore would confuse thought to imply that a sign (for example circumcision) was a type of *anything;* rather it was a *sign* and *seal*. Baptism is *also* a *sign* as all are agreed; each (circumcision and baptism) being equally a sign of spiritual realities (including regeneration), the benefits of which are enjoyed by the "children of Zion" (Ps.149:2) even while here below, but not fully realised and enjoyed until the heavenly Zion itself is reached.

On the other hand, as we consider many of the *types* of the first covenant, we see that they speak to us of, and point us to, eternal and spiritual realities. The temple points to the heavenly temple, the Aaronical high priest points to our great High priest in heaven, and so we could continue to enumerate them. The land of Canaan, being the portion of this earth appointed by God as the place of rest for the nation of Israel, points to the saints' spiritual rest in *this world,* entered into by faith, and their everlasting rest in heaven. Even the natural benefits and inheritance conferred by God upon the Israelites in Canaan (corn and oil and grapes, pasture, sheep, etc. etc.) were of necessity *temporary,* and in turn typified the incorruptible inheritance "that fadeth not away" (whereas these other things *did*) and which are reserved in *heaven* for God's people (1 Peter 1:4). If we were to suggest that Canaan is a Christian's inheritance to-day, it would strike a discord in the otherwise perfect harmony of the economy of God. We must keep everything in its place. The things of time extend from the beginning to the end of time, but the spiritual things extend from eternity to eternity.

RITE OF CIRCUMCISION

Against the background of the foregoing considerations, I will now make reference to that most central particular of the Sinaitic Law, around which most of our discussion turns. I refer to the rite of circumcision. Again, as I have already dealt with this subject fairly fully in an earlier section I do not intend to repeat more of what has been said than may be apposite.

God first of all gave Abraham faith to believe in Him and His promises and an interest in the Covenant of Grace, and then He gave him the sign of circumcision, "a seal of the righteousness of . . . faith" (Rom.4:11). This rite of circumcision was subsequently (430 years later) embodied in the Mosaic ceremonial Law. The Covenant that Abraham was interested in, was the one "that was confirmed . . . of God in Christ" (Gal.3:17).

This rite of circumcision, as God gave it to Abraham, was of the deepest spiritual significance, and it never changed its significance so long as it remained in force. It never was intended as a mark of national identity. Corrupt human nature could not alter God's decree. It is true, and a part of the realism of this discussion, that not *all* Israel were the *true* Israel.

God's command was clear, Abraham and his male infants were to receive the sign of circumcision. When his sons grew up and were able to understand the terms of the Covenant, if they believed, as their father Abraham did, then they should circumcise *their* male infants in turn. And so the nation of Israel should have developed.

It is necessary for us to notice a very important detail in the purposes of God, as revealed to Abraham, with respect to his household, having the most far-reaching significance. A principle, which can be recognised throughout Holy Writ, is the responsibility which rests upon the head of a household. This was true in the Old Testament era, and is equally true in the New Testament era. Not only did God recognise the children of Abraham (as a pattern of all children of believing parents) as included in the Covenant of Grace, *for Abraham's sake,* but He held Abraham responsible for their religious instruction. If his children were to come ultimately to believe, for themselves, in the promises of the Covenant, and in the God of the promises, they had to be *taught* in these things. And God held Abraham *personally responsible* for this most important task. Notice how confidently God speaks of His servant: "I know him, that he will command his children and his household after him, and they shall keep the way of the LORD, to do justice and judgment; that the LORD may bring upon Abraham *that which He hath spoken of him*" (Gen.18:19).

How fascinating is the recognition of the ingredient of God's sovereignty here. The blessing does not proceed from *our endeavours,* but clearly God looks for the performance of those endeavours as an ingredient for the fulfilment of His purposes.

Just as much emphasis is to be placed upon the responsibility of believing parents towards their children *to-day*. Other means have sprung up for the instruction of children, but nothing can supplant this divinely ordained responsibility of parents to instruct. Abraham commanded his children, so should we. "This is His commandment, that we should believe on the name of His Son Jesus Christ" (1 John 3: 23). The command of God to men is to *believe*. If a person believes, it is a mark of obedience ("the obedience of faith" — Rom.16: 26).

Sacred history however shows that a division developed within the nation of Israel, dividing it into what has been described as the spiritual seed and the natural seed of Abraham. Furthermore, due to corrupt human nature, and the predominance of an unbelieving faction in the Jewish race, the aspect of God's revealed will and purpose, in the rite of circumcision, was largely disregarded, and increasingly it was looked upon as a mark of national identity, and proud Israel boasted in the fact that *they* were "the circumcision"; *they* were the people of God. However, only in the case of a *believing* Jew did circumcision carry the full spiritual significance that God intended.

Sufficient has been written elsewhere in this treatise in drawing out the relationship between circumcision and baptism. The sad truth relating to the apostasy of the unbelieving Jews, must not be lost sight of in the corresponding situation in the Christian Church. The sign of baptism in an adult does not, of necessity, guarantee the possession of saving faith by that person, although it is often assumed to do so.

OBSERVATIONS ON MATTERS OF DISAGREEMENT

It now remains for me to highlight the points raised in David Kingdon's book with which I find myself in disagreement.

Kingdon implies that some of the promised blessings of the Covenant of Grace may have been implemented before the advent of Christ, but I think I have advanced adequate reasons for disputing this. Subsequently he states that "the covenant made with Abraham . . . has both a temporal and an eternal aspect, an earthly and heavenly substance". But it is not clear what covenant he is referring to. It cannot be the Covenant of Grace, for *that* does not *have* ''a temporal aspect'' or ''an earthly substance.'' However, some of God's *promises* to Abraham have both. When we think of the promises of God to Abraham, we cannot very well overlook the fact that He promised blessings to him on *several* occasions — as it were by degrees. In Gen.12: 2, 3 God refers to those blessings that relate to Abraham's own person, without any reference to his seed. Then in Gen.15: 1–5 the subject of his seed is introduced. Then in Gen.17:5 God refers to the *extent* of his seed, natural and spiritual, embracing all believers of all nations.

God certainly promised a natural progeny to Abraham, and a place for them to dwell in (Gen. 17:8). This text speaks of ''an everlasting possession'' for the seed of Abraham, but this, as always, is promised on the condition of their obedience. And history shows us how notorious was their failure in this respect. Isaiah laments over this failure in Is.63:18.

As enlarged upon elsewhere in this treatise, God's Covenant of Grace is made with believers in Christ, in other words, with all ordained by God to be given eternal life by Jesus Christ, and so cannot be implemented *apart* from Christ. It was essential for Christ to come into the world in order that the benefits of the Covenant might be implemented. ''Christ Jesus came into the world to save sinners'' (1 Tim.1:15).

Abraham was aware of this. He looked for a city — the heavenly Jerusalem. He was a stranger and a pilgrim on the earth and desired a better country, that is, an heavenly (Heb.11:10, 13, 16 and 12:22).

If we follow Abraham's natural seed into the promised land we find that it leads us to a dead end, for all these things are types and shadows ''patterns of things in the heavens,'' and ''figures of the true'' (Heb.9: 23, 24). If we look for anything more than this, in God's promises to Abraham of temporal blessings, then we will be blurring our evangelical vision, and mistaking the real nature of the Covenant of Grace. The promises annexed to the Covenant, which were universal in character (but not in extent), should not be confused with those blessings associated with, and limited to, the nation of Israel. I believe that in this respect, I have already dealt adequately with the matter of the natural descendants of Abraham and with the limited significance of the geographical land of Canaan.

I have answered the suggestion that circumcision had a national reference, as a mark of national separation to God. The nation as separated by God from the rest of the world had a *typical* spiritual significance *only*.

I have already answered the suggestion that circumcision is a type of regeneration. We would confuse the issue if we were to call that a ''type'' which is so clearly labelled in Scripture as a ''sign'' and a ''seal''. Kingdon's deduction from this erroneous hypothesis, that ''the principle of believers and their seed no longer has covenantal significance'' is consequently also erroneous. The ''age of fulfilment'', as it is related to the Covenant of Grace, is in its fullest realisation the age of glory. However, by God's grace we are able to enjoy some of its first fruits even while here below.

In answer to Kingdon's reference to the circumcision of Abraham's servants (Gen.17:12) sufficient has already been said in principle. I will only add a quotation from Matthew Poole on this Scripture:

> ''Grown persons ... were not to be compelled to be circumcised, but if they refused it, were not to be permitted to dwell in his family, lest they should infect others. ... But as for Abraham's servants ... they were thoroughly instructed in religion (Gen.18: 19) and doubtless did willingly embrace it, and submit to this sacrament''.

The answer to the question ''Have our children an hereditary right to salvation?'' is undoubtedly ''no''. The area in which children fit into the picture is in the area of privilege, ''yet the dogs eat of the crumbs which fall from their master's table'' Matt.15:27. God has not circumscribed the Church within the bounds of the Jewish nation, nor within any other known boundaries. This is one of the ''secret things of God''.

In chapter 4 of his book Kingdon sets himself the task of providing an interpretation of ''believers' baptism'' which does justice to the truly Biblical insights of covenant theology. I believe that on reflection he will agree that this is a rather unhappy statement, and reveals a wrong approach to unprejudiced exposition of the Scripture. Not that I have any quarrel with believers' baptism, as can be verified elsewhere in this treatise, but I suspect that he means more that that, otherwise the remark is unsubstantial. I understand him to mean by "believers' baptism" the whole of his interpretation of the Scriptures regarding this subject. His task appears to be to fit *this,* his preconceived interpretation of what is revealed in the Scriptures regarding the sacrament of Christian baptism; to fit *this* into the pattern of covenant theology. This I consider to be the wrong order of procedure for careful and faithful exegesis.

It surprises me that any paedobaptist would quarrel with the requirement of a profession of repentance and faith, in a person of understanding, before receiving baptism. But regrettably it seems that David Kingdon has come across some difficulty in this connection.

Kingdon then goes on to deal with the relationship between young children of church members and the Covenant, referring to the Passover/Lord's Supper analogy, and also our Lord's dealings with little children. But as I have dealt with these matters fully elsewhere I will say nothing further about them here.

Kingdon's statement that "membership of natural Israel was conditional upon natural birth, whereas membership of the new covenant people is dependent upon re-birth", seems to be a confusing statement. As I have already emphasised the term "new covenant" has a very specific connotation. No doubt he means the new administration of the Covenant of Grace. But then he is not comparing like with like. He is comparing what he calls "membership of the new covenant people" (not a very happy expression) with "membership of natural Israel". But there is no comparison between these. The comparison should have been with those included within the terms of the Covenant of Grace as administered under the Mosaic economy. Then we could say that inclusion within *both* these groups of people depended on the re-birth. I think the confusion of this statement is responsible for what he goes on to say, which is equally confusing: "Both the concept of the remnant and the promise of the new covenant, mark the transference of religion from a nationalistic to an ecclesiastical basis". The concept of the remnant is not restricted to the period of the new covenant, and what is meant by transferring "religion" from a "nationalistic basis" to an "ecclesiastical basis" eludes me. True religion is, and always has been, that which is interwoven with the Covenant of Grace, of which the

Church forms an integral part.

Kingdon also discusses the significance of the baptism administered by John the Baptist, which again I have dealt with fairly fully elsewhere.

"We then that are strong ought to bear the infirmities of the weak, and not to please ourselves. Let every one of us please his neighbour for his good to edification. For even Christ pleased not Himself."

Romans 15:1–3.

THE REFORMED BAPTIST POSITION APPLIED

The subject of this section does not form a part of our enquiry into the *interpretation* of the Biblical doctrine of Christian baptism, with regard to its essential and divinely appointed constitution, which is the objective towards which this treatise as a whole is aimed. Rather, we move away in this section, from *this* aspect of the subject, and consider, not so much the doctrine itself, but rather the *application* of the doctrine; which procedure — first doctrine, and then application — is agreed by all students of the Scriptures to be the truly Biblical method.

Whatever part of divine truth we may at any time happen to be studying, it is an absolutely essential part and purpose of our studies to arrive at as accurate an understanding of God's inspired and infallible Word as is possible for us. The Scriptures are part of the Christian's heritage. God has told us that *all* Scripture has been *given* to us "and is profitable" in every way, and has been given for a particular purpose, namely, "that the man of God may be perfect" (2 Tim.3:17). The highest priority, therefore, for a Christian, is for him to arrive at this *accurate* knowledge of what God has given to us in His Word. The mighty Apollos, although he knew so much, and was able to preach so powerfully, needed more light on "the way of God", and we are told that Aquilla and Priscilla "expounded unto him the way of God more perfectly" (Acts 18:26) — that is, "more accurately", or "more exactly". We are under a divine obligation to understand, what God has spoken in His Word, as *accurately* and *exactly* as we possibly can. This is true for *all* Christians, not just those who go to the theological colleges. But that, as we know, is not the end of the matter.

Having arrived at this *accurate* understanding of a particular aspect of revealed truth, which we happen to be studying, we must *then* consider how it is to be *applied*.

So we can say, at this point, that we have been considering, so far, the Biblical teaching relating to the *doctrine* of Christian baptism. *Now,* I propose to consider the *application* of this doctrine, in the context of the Church. But the way that I propose to do this, is to consider how someone else has done it, who is far more fitted for the task than myself. Fitted in several ways. Partly because he was a minister of a church, and that the church of which he was the minister was a Baptist church. But also I select him to quote from because he belongs to that noble body of God's servants known as ''Puritans'' — the redoubtable John Bunyan.

In the *last* section we considered this doctrine as interpreted by a present-day theologian, who occupies the Reformed Baptist position. In *this* section we consider how the orthodox Baptist interpretation of this doctrine has been applied in the realm of the Christian Church — both the local church, and the universal Church.

It needs scarcely to be said, I suppose, that as John Bunyan was a Baptist, I will not be expecting to find any support, in his teachings, for the paedobaptist understanding of the subject of baptism. Indeed I acknowledge the fact that our doctrinal views differ on this subject, as is manifest from what appears elsewhere in this treatise. My present task, therefore, is not to examine the case that John Bunyan makes out to prove the correctness of his interpretation of the Biblical teaching concerning Christian baptism, but rather as I have already indicated, my task is to examine his *application* of that teaching.

It is not surprising, I think, that we find Bunyan setting his application of this teaching in the context of the Biblical doctrine relating to the *Church*. It is because I am of the opinion that the subject of this treatise cannot be correctly understood without seeing it in relation to the universal Church, that I have devoted a section to this particular aspect. In that section I refer briefly to the fact that the Church to-day is divided, artificially, into several denominations. The distinguishing characteristics associated with these several denominations, and about which Christians have not been able to agree over the past centuries, and still do not agree, relate almost entirely to the Biblical teaching concerning Church polity and Church sacraments, particularly the sacrament of baptism. These disagreements have resulted in Christendom (so called) polarising into various separate denominations, each being persuaded that *their* organisation is the one that enjoys full Scriptural warrant.

This artificial partitioning of the Church has inevitably produced artificial barriers. The separate divisions, or denominations, of the Church, have erected certain barriers to prevent the entrance of the *world* into the Church, but regrettably, man has not been able to devise a barrier which will, at the same time, *exclude* the world and *admit* fellow Christians, except as provided for in the Scriptures.

It is against the background of this dilemma, and the unhappy courses to which it can lead, that John Bunyan views the application of the Baptist teaching on Christian baptism. He views himself primarily and essentially as an individual Christian in the context of a local church. He is aware of the fact that the Word of God is very searching, and very specific, on the subject of a Christian having fellowship with an unbeliever. ''Be not unequally yoked together with unbelievers: for what fellowship hath righteousness with unrighteousness?'' (2 Cor.6:14). This is something that God forbids with regard to His Church, and so we must take what steps God has appointed to safeguard the sanctity of Church communion.

It is here that difficulties arise. With a misguided zeal, our Baptist friends have designed and erected their own barrier and safeguard against the transgression of this invisible dividing line between believer and unbeliever. The barrier which they have erected is water baptism — baptism by immersion. It is at this point that these two important subjects coincide — church polity and the sacrament of Christian baptism. The erection of this barrier of water baptism forms an essential part of Baptist church polity. Without it the church would cease to be a Baptist church.

The views which we are about to consider are not the views of a theorist, but are views that have been hammered out on the anvil of harsh reality and persecution. Having formulated his views on the subject under consideration from a careful study of the

Scriptures, and having put them into practice in his own local church, John Bunyan was subjected to much harassment by his brother Baptist ministers. The bone of contention being that Bunyan did *not* make water baptism a barrier against those seeking membership of his church, whereas his opponents considered it to be a vital part of their church's standing. His opponents held their opinion so strongly that they did not stop short of interfering with the membership of the church of which Bunyan was minister — "not only", says Bunyan, "upon *this* congregation to rend it, but also upon *many others about us,* if peradventure they might break us in pieces, and draw from us disciples after them. . . . And (they) endeavoured to persuade me to break communion with my brethren." (He means his non-Baptist brethren).

I have introduced this extract from Bunyan's remarks in order to sketch in, as it were, the background to the arguments which he goes on to develop and which I am proposing to consider. We can see from this, that he was indeed no mere theorist. He had arrived, with a clear mind, at what he saw to be the correct understanding with regard to the application of this doctrine, and no harsh opposition or persecution would deflect him from what he saw to be right, and which in his opinion harmonised with the analogy of Scripture.

It was because he *had* strong Scriptural warrant to confirm and support his views on this subject, that he held to them so tenaciously, and expressed them so forcibly in his unfolding arguments, which we are going to consider. It will already be quite clear to the reader of this treatise that the disagreement between John Bunyan and his opponents, concerns the matter of admitting people into the fellowship and membership of a local church. *Who* should be admitted? *Who* should be refused? *What* is the factor that shall determine who may be received and who may not? Bunyan's Baptist opponents say it is water baptism — no admission without *that.* Bunyan does not agree with this. He has a better, a divinely appointed, yardstick, to determine those who are worthy of being admitted into communion, as we shall see.

It might, I think, be appropriate to introduce at this point a statement in Bunyan's own words, making clear his high regard for the Church's sacraments, lest anyone might feel that he deals too lightly with what is a divine appointment. Bunyan states his views concerning the sacraments in these words: "I believe that Christ hath ordained but two in His Church, namely, water baptism and the Supper of the Lord; both which are of excellent use to the Church in this world . . . and are, as God shall make them, helps to our faith therein. But I count them not the *fundamentals* of our Christianity, nor grounds or rule to communion with saints. Servants they are, and our mystical ministers, to teach and instruct us in the most weighty matters of the Kingdom of God. I therefore declare my reverent esteem of them; yet dare not remove them, as some do, from the place and end, where by God they are set and appointed; nor ascribe unto them more than they were ordered to have, in their first and primitive institution. It is possible to commit idolatry even with God's own appointments". An example of the way that even God's own appointments may be turned to idolatrous ends is found in the case of the brazen serpent, appointed by God for His people's benefit, and made an object of worship by them to their own undoing (2 Kings 18:4).

Although Bunyan believed wholeheartedly in baptism by immersion he was very much opposed to the practice, which I have just mentioned, of making it a barrier against communion with any saint who had not submitted to it. Let us then now turn to a consideration of Bunyan's treatment of this matter. He explains — "By the word 'communion', I mean fellowship in the things of the Kingdom of Christ, or that which is commonly called 'church communion', the communion of saints".

Having made clear his terms of reference he proceeds to set down his thoughts on this subject under two distinct heads, describing first, those people with whom he dare *not* hold communion, and secondly, those with whom he *dare*. And as this division of the subject seems to assist clear thinking, we will proceed on the same lines.

PEOPLE WITH WHOM BUNYAN DARE NOT HAVE COMMUNION

The people with whom he dare *not* have communion are "them that profess not faith and holiness, or that are not visible saints by calling." Because God has from the beginning commanded this segregation between "the seed of the woman and the children of the wicked" (Gen.3:15) we must take what steps we *can* to comply with His command. Bunyan goes on to say "I dare not have communion with *them* because the example of New Testament churches before us (shows those churches to)* have been a community of visible *saints*. Paul to the Romans writes thus: 'to all that be in Rome, beloved of God, called to be saints:' and to the rest of the churches similarly." Also taking examples from Old Testament history, Bunyan shows how a mingling of believers and unbelievers, in the Old Testament setting, have brought down God's judgments upon His people. "Say to the rebellious, even to the house of Israel, Thus saith the Lord GOD; . . . let it suffice you of all your abominations, in that ye have brought into My sanctuary strangers, uncircumcised in heart —" (Ez.44: 6 & 7). Matthew Poole's interpretation of this Scripture is:— "Let the time you have spent on your sins, your many great sins and abominations, let it be thought enough, nay, too much, as 1 Pet.4:3; do so no more."

THOSE WITH WHOM HE DARE HAVE COMMUNION

Bunyan *then* describes the people with whom he *dare* have communion, and goes on to say, that he dare have communion "with those that are visible saints by calling; with those that by the Word of the Gospel have been brought over to faith and holiness, . . . now", he says, "in order to the discovery of this faith and holiness, and so to fellowship in church communion, I hold it that a faithful relation be made thereof by the party thus to be received; yea, if need be, by witnesses also, for the satisfaction of the church, that she may receive in faith and judgment such as best shall suit her holy profession (Acts 9: 26–28; 1 Cor.16:10; 2 Cor. 8:23). Observe it, these texts do respect extraordinary officers; (Paul, Timotheus and Titus) and yet see that, in order to their *reception* by the church, there was made to the church a faithful relation of the faith and holiness of these very persons; for no man may intrude himself upon, or thrust himself upon, or thrust himself into, a church of Christ, without the church have first the knowledge and liking of the person to be received: if otherwise,

*Author's parenthesis

there is a door opened for all the heretics in the world''. Then he proposes a likely question: ''By what rule would you receive them into fellowship with yourselves?'' to which he gives this answer ''Even by a discovery of their faith and holiness, and their declaration of willingness to subject themselves to the laws and government of Christ in his Church''. Then he proposes another question ''But do you not count, that *by water baptism,* and not otherwise, *that* being the initiating and entering ordinance, they ought to be received into fellowship?'' and this is his answer ''No. For herein lies the mistake, to think, that because in time past baptism was administered upon conversion, that therefore it is the initiating and entering ordinance into church communion; when by the Word no such thing is testified of it. Besides, that it is not so, will be manifest, if we consider the nature and power of such an ordinance''. (namely an initiating and entering ordinance).

Bunyan goes on to mention several people, such as the eunuch, baptised by Philip, Lydia and others; who were not thereby made a member of a local church. ''If baptism were the *initiating* ordinance'', says Bunyan, ''then was he that was baptised *made a member;* made a member of a particular church, by the very *act* of water baptism. Neither ought any, by God's ordinance, to have baptised any, but with respect to the admitting them, *by that act,* to a being of membership in this particular church. For if it *be* the *initiating* ordinance, it *entereth* them into the church. *What* church? Into a visible church. Now, there is no church visible, but that which is particular, the universal (Church) being utterly invisible, and known to none but God. The person then (such as the Ethiopian eunuch) that is baptised, stands *by that* a member of no church at all, neither of the visible nor yet of the invisible. A visible saint he is, but not *made* so by baptism; for he must be a visible saint *before,* else he ought not to be baptised (Acts 8:37; 9:18; 16: 31–33)''.

So we can summarise Bunyan's argument in this way. We find examples in the Bible of cases where a person has submitted to Christian baptism without being thereby, and as the result of *that act,* admitted into the fellowship of a particular local church. And as any particular church is but a local manifestation of the universal Church of Christ, we must conclude that baptism neither makes a person a member of a particular, visible, church, nor of the universal Church, nor does it make that person a visible saint, nor does it give to him any right to, nor being of, membership whatsoever. In other words, baptism is *not* the initiating or entering ordinance for either a visible local church, or the universal Church.

''Now then'', continues Bunyan, ''if baptism be *not* the initiating ordinance, we must seek for entering some other way, by some other appointment of Christ. That which by Christ is made the door of entrance into the Church, by that we may doubtless enter; and seeing baptism is *not* that ordinance, we ought not to seek to enter thereby, but may with good conscience enter without it.''

RULE FOR RECEIVING INTO CHURCH MEMBERSHIP

Here Bunyan proposes another question in order to bring out the point he is making, more clearly: ''By what rule then, would you gather persons into church communion?'' To which question he gives this answer ''Even by that rule by which they are discovered to the *church* to be visible saints, and willing to be gathered into their body and fellowship. By that Word of God, therefore, by which their faith, experience, and conversation, being examined, is found good; by *that* the church should receive them into fellowship with them.'' As circumcision in the *flesh* was the *Old Testament* entering ordinance, so the inward circumcision of the *heart* is the *New Testament* entering ordinance (Rom.2;28,29) When you know a person to have been *thus* circumcised, he ought to be admitted into communion; and this becomes particularly evident when we realise that by the mark of *this* circumcision he is shown to be a citizen in the kingdom of heaven. ''For the Kingdom of God is not meat and drink; (i.e. things ceremonial, ritual and external) but righteousness, and peace, and joy in the Holy Ghost. For he that in these things serveth Christ is acceptable to God, and approved of men (Rom.14:17,18)''.

So Bunyan reiterates his assertion that he will hold communion, the closest communion, with visible saints, whether they *have,* or, for want of light, have *not* submitted to water baptism, and he gives the following four reasons for making this assertion. The *first reason* being — ''Because the true visible saint hath already subjected (himself) to that which is better, even to 'the righteousness of God which is by faith of Jesus Christ' (Rom. 3:22), by which he stands *just* before God; he also hath made *the most exact and strict rule under heaven,* that whereby he squares his life before men. He hath 'like precious faith' with the best of saints, and a conversation according to light received, 'as it becometh the Gospel of Christ' (Ph.1:27). He is therefore to be received. For his *second reason* Bunyan quotes from Ephesians 4:1 – 6 as follows:— '' 'One Spirit, one hope, one Lord, one faith, one baptism (not of water, 'for by one Spirit are we all baptised into one body') one God and Father of all, who is above all, and through all, and in you all,' is a sufficient rule for us to hold communion by, and also to endeavour the maintaining that communion, and to keep it in unity within the bond of peace, against all attempts whatsoever''. Bunyan is here mentioning, in passing, that the word ''baptism'' in Ephesians 4: 5 is referring to the Spirit's work of regeneration, thereby putting a person into the mystical body of Christ, as is expressed also in 1 Cor.12:13.

But in the *third place,* what better reason could we have for holding the closest communion with visible saints than to reflect upon the fact that *God* has communion with them, ''whose example in the case'' says Bunyan ''we are straightly commanded to follow — 'We then that are strong ought to bear the infirmities of the weak, and not to please ourselves. Let everyone of us please his neighbour for his good to edification. For *even Christ* pleased not Himself; but, as it is written, The reproaches of them that reproached Thee fell on Me. For whatsoever things were written aforetime were written for our learning, that we through patience and comfort of the Scriptures might have hope. Now the God of patience and consolation grant you to be likeminded one toward another according to Christ Jesus: that ye may with one mind and one mouth glorify God, even the Father of our Lord Jesus Christ. Wherefore receive ye one another, as Christ also received us to the glory of God' (Rom.15:1 – 7)''. This surely is an irresistible reason.

Bunyan, addressing his remarks to one of his opponents in this debate; one who contends for the necessity of a person's submitting to water baptism before being admitted into church communion; says, ''Think not by the straightness of thine order, in outward and bodily conformity to outward and shadowish circumstances, that thy peace is maintained with God; for peace with God is by faith in the blood of His cross, who hath borne the reproaches of you both. Wherefore he that hath communion with God for Christ's sake, is as good and as worthy of the communion of saints as thyself. *God* hath received him, *Christ* hath received him, therefore do *you* receive him.'' Bunyan asks the question: ''If notwithstanding *thy great* sins thou standest, by Christ, complete before *the throne of God,* why may not your *brother,* notwithstanding his *little ones* (concerning baptism) stand complete before *thee* in the church?''

Another reason, the *fourth reason* that Bunyan gives for holding communion with such a brother, is because the edification of souls in the faith and holiness of the Gospel should be of greater concernment with us (it was with him) than an agreement in outward things. Not only should it be of more concernment with us, but also it would be of far more *profit* to our brother, than our agreeing in, or contesting for, the business of water baptism. When Paul was handling another tricky subject in the church at Corinth, the matter of eating things offered to idols, many in that church knew that ''an idol is nothing'', but the matter was troubling some. Paul said ''Knowledge puffeth up, but charity edifieth'' (1 Cor.8:1,4). Bunyan says, ''That the edification of the soul is of the greatest concern, is out of measure evident, because heaven and eternal happiness are so immediately concerned therein. Besides this, the edification of the soul, is that for which Christ died, for which the Holy Ghost was given, yea, for which the Scriptures are given to the Church. But to contest with gracious men, with men that walk with God; to shut such out of the churches, because they will not sin against their souls, (by acting against their convictions or without light), rendereth thee uncharitable – 'if thy brother be grieved with thy meat, now walkest thou not charitably. Destroy not him with thy meat, for whom Christ died. . . . For meat destroy not the work of God. All things indeed are pure; but it is evil for that man who eateth with offence' (Rom.14: 15 & 20). Let us therefore leave off these contentions, and 'follow after the things which make for peace, and things wherewith one may edify another' (Rom.14:19), and know, that the edification of the Church of God dependeth not upon, neither is tied to, this or that circumstance (he is of course referring to the matter of baptism as a 'circumstance'). Especially when there are, in the hearts of the godly, different persuasions about it, then it becometh them (all parties), in the wisdom of God, to take more care for their peace and unity, than to widen or make large their uncomfortable differences.''

EXAMPLES FOUND IN THE BIBLE

In order to give support to the principles which he has been underlining in the above quotation, Bunyan refers to a number of examples out of the Bible where laws and ordinances of old have been broken, and the breach of them borne with, when the profit and edification of the people of God came in competition with them. These examples include the case, in Leviticus 10:16—20, of Aaron transgressing the ceremonial Law, ''Because he ate not the sin offering of the people, yet seeing that he could not do it with satisfaction to his own conscience, Moses was content that he left it undone''. Again Bunyan quotes the case of Hezekiah, as recorded in 2 Ch.30:13 to 27, where we read at verse 18 that some did 'eat the passover otherwise than it was written'. ''Yet'', says Bunyan, ''the wise king would not forbid them, but rather admitted it, knowing that their edification was of greater concern than to hold them to a circumstance or two. Yea, God Himself did like the wisdom of the king, and *'healed'*, that is, 'forgave' the people at the prayer of Hezekiah''. And again, Bunyan remarks — ''When Christ's disciples plucked the ears of corn on the sabbath, no doubt for very hunger, and were rebuked by the Pharisees for it, as for that which was unlawful, how did their Lord succour them? By *excusing* them, and rebuking their adversaries: ''Have ye not read what David did, when he was an hungred, and they that were with him; how he entered into the house of God, and did eat the shewbread, which was not lawful for him to eat, neither for them which were with him, but only for the priests? Or have ye not read in the law, how that on the sabbath days the priests in the temple profane the sabbath, and are blameless?' (see Matt. 12:1–5). Why blameless? Because they did it in order to the edification of the people.''

In passing, and in order to grasp a little more clearly, the principle lying behind this incident of the disciples plucking ears of corn on the sabbath day, it should be observed that the Lord

Jesus, in justifying their action, shows that the principle involved is the same as that underlying David's contravening a point of the Jewish ceremonial Law, relating to the shewbread. It involved a distinguishing between the *letter* of the Law and the *intent* of the Law. Commenting on this, David Dickson remarks: "When the mind of the Lawgiver and the intent and the end of the command, is not contravened, the precept is not broken. Not reading nor considering the Scripture, whereby the meaning of the Law may be understood, is the cause of error and mistaking of duties."

In the light of the above mentioned examples, Bunyan reasons the matter out like this. "If, in this way, laws and ordinances of old have been broken, and the breach of them borne with, when the profit and edification of the people came in competition, how much *more* may not we have communion, church communion, where no law is transgressed thereby?"

This line of thought seems to lead naturally to the principle of love between brethren. "Love", says Bunyan, "which above all things we are commanded to *put on,* is of much more worth than to break about baptism. — 'above all these things put on charity, which is the bond of perfectness' (Col.3:14). Love is sometimes *more seen and showed* in forbearing to urge and press what we know, than in publishing and imposing. 'I could not', said Paul, love would not let me, 'speak unto you as unto spiritual, but as unto carnal, even as unto babes in Christ. I have fed you with milk, and not with meat: for hitherto ye were not able to bear it, neither yet now are ye able' (1 Cor.3:1 & 2). To make an outward circumstance the door to fellowship which God hath not; yea, to make that *including, excluding charter,* the bounds, bar, and rule of communion, when by the Word of the everlasting testament there is no warrant for it; to speak charitably, if it be not for want of love, it is for want of knowledge in the mysteries of the Kingdom of Christ. Take two Christians, equal in *all points but this,* nay, let one go beyond the other far, for grace and holiness; yet this circumstance of water shall drown and sweep away *all* his excellences, not counting him worthy of that reception that with hand and heart shall be given to a novice in religion, because he consents to water".

Bunyan, in viewing the church scene of his day, saw how this matter of water baptism had erected barriers between brethren, and had divided the Church of Christ (which was, and is, one) into parties, presenting a pathetic scene to the world, of bickering and contending brethren. Christ never intended His Church to be divided, not even into denominations. Notice how Bunyan regarded this sorry sight:— "For God's people to divide into parties" he says "or to shut each other from church communion, though from *greater* points, and upon *higher* pretences, than this of water baptism, hath heretofore been counted carnal, and the actors herein babyish Christians. Paul and Apollos, Cephas and Christ, were doubtless higher "things" than those about which *we* contend; yet when they made divisions for *them*, how sharply are they rebuked! 'For whereas there is among you envying, and strife, and divisions, (or factions) are ye not carnal?' (1 Cor.3:3)".

Bunyan says that his great concern in all this is "to persuade my brethren of the baptised way not to hold too much thereupon, not to make baptism an essential of the Gospel of Christ, nor yet of communion of saints. 'Christ sent me not be baptise' (1 Cor.1:17). These words are spoken with holy indignation against them that abused this ordinance of Christ. So when he speaketh of the ministers themselves, which also they had abused; in his speaking, he, as it were, trampled upon them, as if they were nothing at all: 'Who then *is* Paul?' and 'Who *is* Apollos?' (1 Cor.3:5). Yet for all this, the ministers and their ministry are a glorious appointment of God in the world. Baptism also is a holy ordinance; but when Satan abuseth it and wrencheth it out of its place, making that which was ordained of God for the *edification* of believers, the only weapon to break in pieces the love, the unity, the concord of saints, then what *is* baptism? Then neither is *baptism* anything" (in the same sense as Paul had been saying "Neither is he that *planteth* anything" etc. 1 Cor. 3:7) "And this is no new doctrine;" says Bunyan "for God, by the mouth of his prophets of old, cried out against His own institutions, when *abused* by His people: 'To what purpose is the multitude of your sacrifices unto Me? saith the LORD: I am full of the burnt offerings of rams, and the fat of fed beasts; and I delight not in the blood of bullocks, or of lambs, or of he goats. When ye come to appear before Me, who hath required *this* at your hand, to tread My courts?' (Is.1:11 & 12) And yet *all these were His own appointments*. But why then did He thus abhor them? Because they used them as they did other of His appointments, namely 'For strife and debate, and to smite with the fist of wickedness' (Is. 58:4)''.

Bunyan is evidently dismayed by the practice of some of his Baptist brethren of excluding Christians from church communion, and of debarring them from their heaven born privileges, ''for the want of that which God never made a wall of division between us''. He then enumerates a number of implications of this attitude as he sees it, and I will mention some of them.

''It respecteth more the *form,* than the spirit and *power* of godliness (2 Tim.3:5). This is to make laws where God hath made none. It bindeth all men's faith to ''*my* opinion''. It taketh away the children's bread. It holdeth staggering consciences in doubt of the right way of the Lord. It abuseth the Holy Scriptures; it wresteth God's ordinances out of their places.''

Some may be surprised that such a well known Baptist minister should express his thoughts so strongly on this subject. I think that our general respect for John Bunyan, and his evident clear understanding of the doctrines of grace as declared in the Holy Scriptures, will *oblige* us to give consideration to the views which he has expressed regarding the Scriptural teaching of Christian baptism, and particularly its application to the life of the local church. As will be understood, the observations and reasonings, which I have been dwelling on at some length, including very full quotations, so as to avoid the danger of my conveying the wrong impression, or placing a wrong emphasis at any point, *these* represent Bunyan's case for ''daring (as he says) to have communion with a true Christian who, nevertheless, for legitimate personal reasons, had not submitted to water baptism.'' He knew that many of his brother ministers in other Baptist churches forbad such communion. Consequently he found himself a reluctant contestant in a controversy arising from, and centring upon, a difference of understanding regarding this matter.

The background to this discussion might be better appreciated if we were to notice what Bunyan had to say in his letter to the reader. The following extract helps to convey something of this background:— ''I had not set pen to paper about this controversy had we been let alone at quiet in our Christian communion. But being assaulted for more than sixteen years, wherein the brethren of the baptised way (as they had their opportunity) have sought to break us in pieces, merely because we are not, in their way, or baptised first. . . . That I deny the ordinance of baptism, or that I have placed one piece of an argument against it, though they fain it, is quite without colour or truth. All I say is, that the church of Christ hath not warrant to keep out of their communion the Christian that is discovered to be a visible saint by the Word; the Christian that walketh according to his light, with God.''

Bunyan's insistence upon this point is understandable, and would appear to be warrantable, when we bear in mind the teaching of the Lord Jesus Christ in John's Gospel chapter 10 verses 1 – 16. There he depicts all the members of the true Church of God as sheep in a sheepfold, and He Himself as the door. ''I am the door''. The ''I'' is emphatic, meaning ''I alone''. There simply is no other entrance. Not even baptism. He is the sole entrance into the true Church, and so also into local churches, which are local manifestations of the true universal Church.

RELATIONSHIP OF BAPTISM TO THE LAW

One important part of Bunyan's understanding of this subject, and which has not been touched on so far, relates to the matter of Law. It is agreed that baptism is an ordinance of the Lord Jesus Christ. He commanded His people to be baptised. Now on account of the fact that Bunyan, in his interpretation of the Biblical teaching regarding water baptism, adopts a lenient attitude towards sincere and visible saints who have not been baptised; on account of *this,* his opponents criticise him for seeming to condone a failure to *obey* this command. The question they put to Bunyan is this: ''Is baptism none of the laws of Christ?'' To this, Bunyan gives the following answer — ''It is none of those laws, neither any part of them, that the Church, *as a church,* should show her obedience by. For albeit that baptism be given by Christ our Lord to the Church, yet not for them to worship Him by *as a church.* Again, (the suggestion) that submitting to water baptism is a sign that was ever required by any of the primitive churches, of him that would hold fellowship with them, I find not in all the Bible. I find not that baptism is a sign to any but the person that is baptised. The church hath her satisfaction of the person *from better proof.* Baptism makes you no member of the Church, neither doth it make thee a visible saint: it giveth thee therefore, neither right to, nor being of, membership at all.'' Then addressing his remarks somewhat directly and personally, to those who were opposed to him, he says: ''You make the moral Law none of Christ's but Moses'; not the Son's but the servant's. Know you not yet, that a difference is to be put betwixt those rules that discover the essentials of holiness, and those that in themselves are not such; and that that of *faith and the moral Law* is the *one,* and baptism etc., the *other*? Is not love to God, abhorrence of idols, to forbear blaspheming, to honour our parents, to do no murder, to forbear theft, not to bear false witness, nor covet etc.; are not, *these* I say, the precepts of the Lord Jesus because delivered by Moses? (Implying — ''Yes they *are* the precepts of the Lord Jesus''). Or are *these* such as may better be broken, than, for want of light, to forbear baptism with water? Or doth a man, while he liveth in the neglect of *these* (to honour our parents etc.), and in the meantime bustles about those you call Gospel commands (referring of course to water baptism), most honour Christ, or best fit himself for fellowship with the saints? Need I tell you, that the faith of Christ, with the ten commandments, are as much now Gospel commands as baptism; and ought to be in as much, and far more, respect, with the holy ones, than *that,* or other the like. Baptism will neither *admit* a man into fellowship, nor *keep* him there, if he be a transgressor of the moral precept; and again, need I tell you, that a man who believeth in Jesus, and fulfilleth the royal Law, doth more glorify God, and honour religion in the world, than he that keepeth (if there *were* so many) ten thousand figurative laws.'' (Such as baptism).

SUMMARY

Gathering all up into a summary statement, Bunyan says to his opponents: ''When you have *proved* that water baptism, which you yourself have said is not a church ordinance, is *essential* to church communion, and that the church may, *by the Word of God,* bolt, bar, and for ever shut out those, far better than ourselves, that have *not,* according to our notion, been baptised with water, then it will be time enough to talk of ground for so doing. In the meantime I must take leave to tell you, there is not in all the Bible one syllable for such a practice, wherefore your great cry about your order is wordless, and therefore faithless, and is a mere human invention''.

I have thus set before the reader of this treatise, a Scripturally based argument, extracted from papers published by John Bunyan in reply to those who chose to contend vigorously with him, with regard to the place which water baptism should occupy in the worship, fellowship, life, discipline and order of a particular local church. This he did *partly* to avoid the impression that silence might leave in the minds of people, in relation to the published arguments of his opponents, that there was *no answer* to them. But *partly* he published a reason for his *own* practice so as to settle his brethren, with whom he enjoyed communion and fellowship, and to arm them against the attempts, which he knew were being made by his brother Baptist ministers, to unsettle them in their convictions, and their sense of peace with God, with regard to this matter.

''Behold, how good and how pleasant it is for brethren to dwell together in unity!''
Psalm 133:1.

''Now the God of peace, that brought again from the dead our Lord Jesus, that great Shepherd of the sheep, through the blood of the everlasting Covenant, make you perfect in every good work to do His will, working in you that which is wellpleasing in His sight, through Jesus Christ; to whom be glory for ever and ever. Amen.''
Hebrews 13:20, 21.

CONCLUSION

I have endeavoured, in the foregoing pages, to bring together all the most relevant Scriptures that bear upon the subject of baptism; opening up their radical meaning and thereby identifying certain broad, balanced, and Scripturally based principles, relating to God's great plan of redemption, so as to relate the subject of baptism *to* that plan, and to those principles.

It is most important that we place the chief emphasis where it should be placed. I have, in the course of this discussion, tried to paint in, as it were, the scenario of God's great plan of redemption, and to see the central subject of our discussion in *that* context. Going back to the beginning of time we glimpsed at the perfection of God's creation, the tragedy of the Fall and the inevitable doom of man, if left to himself. We saw how God broke into that scene of doom with a declaration of His unmerited favour to some, as embodied in His promise of salvation. God broke through the stormy clouds of judgment with an announcement of mercy to guilty sinners. We have seen how this declaration of God's mercy was presented in the form of a covenant — the Covenant of Grace. More than 2000 years went by after its first promulgation, during which time the natural wickedness of the human heart had revealed itself to such an extent that Moses recorded the situation in this way: ''GOD saw that the wickedness of man was great in the earth, and that every imagination of the thoughts of his heart was only evil continually'' (Gen.6:5). But God did not forget His Covenant. His hand of judgment fell on the race of men, but He preserved a remnant in Noah and his family. After another 3½ centuries God called Abram out of all the families of the earth to be the head of His chosen race, the Jews. Not only the natural head of the Jewish nation, but also the father of the spiritual race of all the faithful in all ages, to the end of time.

At this stage, in the days of Abraham, God made a further development in His Covenant, manifesting *even more* grace, by ordaining a *sign* and a *seal* of the Covenant, thus making the promise *more sure* to poor doubting, trembling, sinners: ''to the end the promise might be sure to all the seed; not to that only which is of the Law, but to that also which is of the faith of Abraham; who is the father of us all'' says the apostle Paul (Rom.4: 16).

I have emphasised the importance of recognising the continuity of the Covenant of Grace. It was not a covenant just for the Jews, which came to an end at the introduction of the Christian era; but it has continued, in its applicability, right up to the present time, and it will continue to be applicable to believing sinners, on to the end of time. This Covenant that God confirmed to Abraham is the Covenant that contains that priceless and indispensible promise that we find recorded for us in John 3: 16.

God did not change the Covenant at the introduction of the Christian era, but once again made a further development of it, manifesting therein *even more* grace. He changed the sign and seal of the Covenant from one that involved the shedding of blood (circumcision) to the bloodless sign and seal of baptism. An exact parallel of the change from the sacrament of the sacrificial paschal lamb to the bloodless sacrament of the Lord's Supper. But not only that. God displayed *even more* of His grace by manifesting to the sight of human eyes the Redeemer, promised in the first promulgation of the Covenant, in the Garden of Eden, when He made the divine declaration that Satan would bruise His heel and the Redeemer would inflict upon Satan a mortal blow — which He did on the Cross of Calvary — (Gen.3: 15; Col.2: 14, 15).

I urge all those who read these lines to meditate upon what I have put before you regarding God's Covenant of Grace. I think we must all agree that we are living in spiritually dangerous days. Peter has given a warning to God's people for just such a time as this: ''Be sober, be vigilant; because your adversary the devil, as a roaring lion, walketh about, seeking whom he may devour'' (1 Peter 5: 8). The devil is active to-day, and the subject of his malice, and the target of his attack, is Christ and His Church; and he knows that one of the most successful ways of making inroads into the ranks of God's people is to cause them to be so preoccupied with their own internal and domestic disputes that their thoughts and their meditations are diverted from a contemplation of God's "exceeding great and precious promises (2 Pet.1:4)", and of His glory.

Brethren, let us look away for a moment from our ecclesiastically entrenched positions. Some of us (we who are God's redeemed people), some of us are in *one* denomination and some are in *another,* feeling no doubt, in certain cases, that we cannot possibly surrender an inch of the ground on which we stand, lest we find that we are compromising with error. Fear has gripped us, and almost paralysed our powers of thinking, and we are hemmed in to an inevitable line of reasoning which suggests to us that our fathers in the faith established for ever our particular ecclesiastical position, several centuries ago, when they felt obliged to separate from other brethren on doctrinal grounds due to a failure to agree on a common ecclesiastical basis. I suggest that we are often fearful of moving our position because we are convinced that our founding fathers were right in everything that they did and said. On account of this we find the Church to-day segregated into many denominations, each standing upon, and continuing in existence on account of, certain differences of interpretation of Scripture.

Thomas Witherow seems to have expressed this line of thought very well. He first of all says this:— "The various forms of church Government that we find existing at present in the Christian world may be classed under some one or other of these three heads:— PRELACY, INDEPENDENCY, and PRESBYTERY". Then he goes on to say:— "Which, then, of the three forms of church Government prevalent through the world is it the duty of a Christian to select and to support?

"This is a question of great importance. It is, besides, forced upon our consideration in every locality where a dissenting chapel lifts its front, and a church steeple tapers into air. And yet it must be admitted, that the majority of Christians contrive to pass through life without ever giving an hour's thought to this most interesting theme. Most people are content to let their ancestors choose a church for them, and every Sabbath walk to Divine worship in the footsteps of their great-grandfathers—they know not why, and care not wherefore. Some shrink from inquiry, lest it should turn out that the church to which they are bound by ties of family, education, and habit, is destitute of all Scriptural authority, and lest they feel uncomfortable by having their convictions and their interests set at war''.*

When we look into God's Word, we find declared there, in the clearest terms, that God's people are involved in a warfare; ''not against flesh and blood, but against principalities, against powers, against the rulers of the darkness of this world'' (Eph.6: 12). I say *we are involved* in it. But are we *engaged* in it? Whether we realise it or not we *are* involved in it. Nothing is more important in this connection than to identify our enemy; then we can be prepared to offer resistance. And nothing better promotes that resistance than for God's people to close their ranks, to recognise that God has broken down that crucial middle wall of partition between Jew and Gentile, the classical and representative division of all our credal boundaries, and so has established a principle that never again must man-made barriers be erected to divide God's people, for ''we, being many, are one body in Christ, and every one members one of another'' (Rom.12: 5) ''— whether we be Jews or Gentiles, whether we be bond or free . . .'' (1 Cor.12: 13); whether we be *this* denomination or *that,* it makes no difference. ''What therefore God hath joined together, let not man put asunder'' (Matt.19: 6). There is only *one* entrance ticket into Christ's Church and that is personal, trusting, cleaving, faith in the Lord Jesus Christ as Saviour, and acknowledgment of Him as Lord. No walls of partition; all ranks should be closed and knit together, so that we measure up to that divinely inspired description of the Church, as we face together our *real* enemy, and fight the *Lord's* battles: ''Thou art beautiful, O my love, as Tirzah, comely as Jerusalem, terrible as an army with banners'' (Song 6: 4).

I have urged you to meditate upon what I have already put before you regarding God's Covenant. I have done so, lest there be some who still have some doubts about it. This is of course not the place for me to expand upon that subject, I have done that already; but here I simply emphasise the centrality of the teaching of the Covenant in the whole of the Bible. After the destroying

*Extract from *'The Apostolic Church. Which is it?'* First published 1967.

judgment of the Flood, God re-established His Covenant with Noah (Gen.6: 18). Then about 450 years later God said to Abraham "I will establish My Covenant with him (Isaac) for an everlasting Covenant" (Gen.17: 19). "God", said David, "hath made with me an everlasting Covenant, ordered in all things, and sure: for this is all my salvation, and all my desire" (2 Sam.23: 5).

I think that sufficient has been said to establish the principle that, "according to the purpose of Him who worketh all things after the counsel of His own will" (Eph.1: 11), and "according to the riches of His grace" (Eph.1: 7), God has determined to give His people confirmation of His merciful purposes towards guilty sinners in the form of a Covenant. We cannot but see the parallel between this and what we find in Heb.6: 17—20 "Wherein God, willing more abundantly to shew unto the heirs of promise the immutability of his counsel, confirmed it by an oath: that by two immutable things, in which it was impossible for God to lie, we might have a strong consolation, who have fled for refuge to lay-hold upon the hope set before us: which hope we have as an anchor of the soul, both sure and stedfast, and which entereth into that within the veil; whither the forerunner is for us entered, even Jesus, made an high priest for ever after the order of Melchisedec". Truly God looked on the promulgation of His Covenant as having the nature and solemnity of an oath, as is evident in His words to Abraham: "By myself have I sworn, saith the LORD, . . . that in blessing I will bless thee, . . . and in thy seed shall all the nations of the earth be blessed" (Gen.22: 16 – 18). Clearly pointing to the "seed" of Gal. 3:16.

With this established principle therefore behind us, let us move on to a final glance at that which God has annexed to His Covenant of Grace, namely the seals. For more than 2000 years God's redeemed people found assurance of His promises of mercy in the naked words of the God "with whom is no variableness, neither shadow of turning" (Jas.1: 17). And then to add to His display of grace He introduced something to confirm the Covenant — God determined to be gracious to sinners — He confirmed His purposes of grace in terms of a Covenant. Then He confirmed His Covenant by ordaining a *seal* to be annexed to it, giving the sign and seal of circumcision to Abraham and his male seed. Surely! (we might gasp) how much further could He go?

What more could He have done? — ''What could have been done more to My vineyard, that I have not done in it?'' (Isaiah 5:4).

It is at this point that we must watch the hand of God very closely. God determined, and made clear beyond any doubt, that in His Covenant of Grace, which He had confirmed to Abraham, it was His will that the infant seed of His believing people should be included within the terms of the Covenant, and this appears to have been a further clarification of God's gracious provisions for His people in *all* ages, because their children were *a part of themselves,* the fruit of their bodies, bearing the very closest affinity with them. What more natural, and infinitely gracious, than for God's arrangement for His Church to be such that the children of His people should continue to be recognised as *part of them,* and so bear the sign and seal of the Covenant as well. The babies born to His people were not, as it were, cast out into the unbelieving heathen world, of which Satan is the prince, but they were considered as being within the Church, and, federally holy, so as to enjoy the benefits which it was uniquely fitted to afford, as elaborated upon earlier.

There is no doubt that an exact parallel of this principle is seen in the Christian family circle, where the children have the benefit of being brought up in the ''nurture and admonition of the Lord'' (Eph.6: 4). In neither case, in the Church or in the home, is the benefit imparted a *saving* benefit. This then is the situation relating to God's purposes in His Covenant as it was clearly manifest when the Covenant was confirmed to Abraham.

Whereas there is no Scriptural evidence that infants of believing parents *were* included within the Covenant from the *beginning* of time, when God first made known the terms of the Covenant; neither is there any Scriptural evidence that such was *not* always the rule. Furthermore, we have already had occasion to take notice of the invariableness of God, and specifically with respect to His ''every good gift'' (Jas. 1:17). We have watched the way in which God, over the years and centuries, expands and makes clearer and fuller His Covenant; but nothing that He has said gives us reason to believe that He has ever changed the description of the beneficiaries of His Covenant confirmed to Abraham, which is for the benefit of believing parents and their seed.

We have seen already that whereas the sign and seal of the

Covenant in the *Jewish* era was that of *circumcision*, the sign and seal of the Covenant in the *Christian* era is *baptism*. Is this a stumbling block with any who may be reading these words? In deference to those who are in difficulty at this point let us pause to consider it. I assume that we have no difficulty in accepting the principle of God having declared and confirmed His purposes of grace in terms of a Covenant. Neither does there seem to be any difficulty in recognising a further display of God's grace, in the *adding* of a sign and a seal to the Covenant, in the form of circumcision. It would seem to be introducing a difficulty if we were to say that in this Christian era God had taken a step backward, and had withdrawn from His people a seal and a sign of His Covenant. So we must not say*that*. We must rather say that His people continue to *have* a sign. We know that the sign of circumcision has been abolished, so we now look for another sign, and what else could it be but the sign of baptism?

If we are agreed that baptism has been appointed by God as the sign and seal of the Covenant in this Christian era in the place of circumcision, what do we say about the children of believing parents? How do *they* fit into the context of the Covenant? Are they included? Or are they excluded? It would seem that the argument drawn from the parallel situation in the Jewish era is quite irresistible. We have seen what gracious provision God made for children of believing parents at *that* time, and the benefits which God ordained for *them*, although they were not necessarily saving benefits — (they were for Isaac: but not for Ishmael). I assume however that we accept the fact that they were *real* benefits, and that they were established and provided by a divine command. Then would it not be unreasonable and unGodlike, for God to withhold those benefits from believing parents and their children in this Christian era? We might well exclaim with faithful Abraham: "That be far from Thee to do after this manner" (Gen.18: 25). We must therefore conclude that the same benefits of the Covenant as were enjoyed by Abraham and his infants, are in fact conferred upon the infants of believing parents in this Gospel age, and that they must therefore receive the sign of the Covenant — baptism — as symbolising their inclusion within the Covenant, together with their parents.

If there are still some of you who stumble at the idea of infants being baptised, let us try to look at your difficulties in the light of the foregoing, and in the light of what is revealed to us in the Scriptures of the character of God. What is the real difficulty? Are you not satisfied with the arguments which I have placed before you regarding the Covenant? But whether we call it a covenant or a testament we must all be agreed that the promises of God are the sheet anchor of the believer's soul. And the Covenant simply comprehends and ratifies those promises. Is it the notion of a sign and a seal which is the difficulty?, and their relation to faith? Paul says that Abraham ''received the sign of circumcision, a seal of the righteousness of the faith which he had yet being uncircumcised: that he might be the father of all them that believe, though they be not circumcised'' (Rom.4: 11). It cannot be denied that the infant seed of Abraham also received this sign as well as Abraham. We must conclude therefore from the very character of God, that God still holds in His heart the same affectionate feelings towards the children of believing parents in *this* age, as He did do in Abraham's age.

What then is the difficulty? Do you object that such teaching eclipses the importance of adult baptism? For, surely, (you may reason,) was not this the very thing that the people were exhorted to by Peter on the Day of Pentecost? But this teaching does *not exclude* adult baptism, nor eclipse its importance. Whenever an adult person is converted from unbelief to the Christian faith by the regenerating power of God's Spirit, such a person is a proper subject for baptism, and indeed comes under the divine command to be baptised, provided they were not baptised in infancy. If however they had been baptised in infancy they would already have received the seal of the Covenant, and as is so clearly demonstrated in the case of the seal of circumcision, the seal cannot be received *twice.*

Other possible objections have already been considered, and it would be pointless to enumerate them here; I merely exhort any one who may still stumble at the arguments herein propounded, in support of the practice of administering baptism to infants, to make quite sure that the teaching on which you base *your* views is derived from clear Scriptural exposition. Not simply from a few isolated Scriptures, but in accordance with the analogy of faith and the consistent tenor of ''all the counsel of God'' (Acts 20:27). I entreat you to look again at all the Scriptures that have been cited in this treatise, which relate to the subject before us, because if there remains any disagreement between us (and my earnest desire and longing is that such differences should by now have melted away) then such disagreement can only be concerning the interpretation of the Scriptures.

Whenever we deal with subjects such as the one before us, concerning which different views are held by God's people, there is always a danger that prejudice and preconceived ideas surreptitiously worm their way into the argument being propounded. Where this happens, and is undetected, any benefit that might otherwise be derived from the argument is largely neutralised, and the argument in turn discredited. It has therefore been my earnest endeavour, in compiling this treatise, to avoid any such intrusions of erroneous and misleading prejudice; but remembering how frail we all are, (Ps.39:4) and fallible children of the dust, some "intruders" may have slipped in unawares; in which case I would welcome their discovery, and would esteem such discovery to be a means of detecting and eliminating error, and contributing towards the establishment of a firm and universally acceptable basis, upon which to rest our understanding of this most important subject, Christian baptism.

How prone we all are to prejudice. It is in our very nature. God has given to us an enduring illustration of it in the case of the Jews' prejudice in favour of their own religion, and in particular with regard to the matter of circumcision, and its presumed continuing necessity for salvation — "certain men which came down from Judea taught the brethren, and said, Except ye be circumcised after the manner of Moses, ye cannot be saved" (Acts 15:1).

The infant Christian Church *nipped this error in the bud.* The unresolved disagreement in the more adult Christian Church today, concerning the doctrine of Christian baptism, is a spiritual canker undermining its life and witness. It would seem that there is an urgent case for searching the Scriptures again, to discover the Holy Spirit's mind in this matter.

I would now address a few final remarks to those of you who occupy what we may call the traditional Baptist position, with regard to this subject of baptism. I understand that you will tell me that to go down into the water with a profession of faith and repentance is the very turning point in a person's religious life. You say, I believe, that when you have gone down into the water you have taken the first step towards heaven. I would not say that *all* Baptists hold these opinions, but I believe that many do. Now it seems to me that such opinions exalt baptism to a position of prominence in the economy of God such that God never intended it to occupy. Let us readily acknowledge that to receive the sign and seal of baptism is something commanded by God; a command to which we owe obedience. But the *whole* of God's revelation demands obedience; the obedience of faith and the obedience of works. Let us suppose, for the sake of our discussion, the opinion which you hold is wrong. Many greatly respected interpreters of the Scriptures, in past periods of the Church's history, do not share your interpretation. What if your opinion is wrong? Where would this leave you? Does your whole spiritual position stand or fall with your interpretation of the Scriptural teaching on the subject of baptism? *That,* I think, is the test.

Does your view of baptism take into account the unity and continuity of the Church from the beginning to the end of time? Do you accept the teaching relating to the Covenant of Grace as outlined in this treatise, and found in the Scriptures? Do you recognise baptism to be a sign and seal of the Covenant? What do you consider to be the position (spiritually) of those saints such as Enoch, who lived before Abraham, and concerning whom, although benefiting from the Covenant, there is no Scriptural evidence of any Covenant sign or seal having been ordained or administered to them? As far as we can tell, they were neither circumcised nor baptised, but they had saving faith, as we are told concerning Enoch (Heb.11: 5). I am raising these specific questions because they seem to me to be germane to the subject before us, and if prayerfully faced up to, may lead us a little nearer to common ground.

In writing this treatise my endeavour has been to search out, and set down, the essential meaning of the text, or where the meaning is not made clear by a particular text, to make reference to this fact. In order that those holding views other than those which I have set before you, may move a little closer to agreement and to common ground, I exhort you, my brethren in Christ, to examine the Scriptural basis of your views again, to make absolutely sure that the Scriptures are bearing their intended meaning. ''Let every man be fully persuaded in his own mind'' (Rom.14: 5).

Whatever else one might think about Puritan divines, one could never accuse them of shallow thinking. And yet we find among them those who occupied one or other of the two main positions relating to this subject of baptism. Among those who took the view generally set out in this treatise were John Owen and John Flavel. Owen was probably one of the greatest theologians of all time, and Flavel was one whose reputation as a theologian and a pastor was held very high in the esteem of his contemporary Puritans. John Bunyan who occupied the Baptist position, was so greatly revered by his fellow Puritans, and is so well known, that no further word of mine is needed. All these men sought to work together in harmony, and men occupying either position were mutually acceptable to each other, provided they embraced the essential doctrines of grace. It is a happy thought, as we have considered at some length in an earlier section, that John Bunyan, a pastor of a Baptist church, was nevertheless content to have paedobaptists as members of that church.

In the whole field of theological discussion, about *this* there can be *no* disagreement; there is only *one* truth which God *intended* His Word to convey in relation to this subject. Christian baptism has only *one* significance in the sight of God, for *He* ordained it, and it is *that* significance which we are *all* concerned to determine. Let us be charitable to each other; our objective is not to contend for a ''party line'', but to discover the truth. That surely is what we *all* want to do.

Let us be resolved to break down all man-made barriers between brethren, all man-made prejudices which have, by the accretion of the centuries, acquired the quality of intractability, unshakability and dogmatism, which ''conversation'' is not such as ''becometh the gospel of Christ'' (Phil.1:27).

''I beseech you, brethren, by the name of our Lord Jesus Christ, that ye all speak the same thing, and that there be no divisions among you; but that ye be perfectly joined together in the same mind and in the same judgment'' (1 Cor. 1: 10). In spite of all existing entrenched positions, which to depart from, if found to be erroneous, needs much grace, let us all take a fresh look at God's Holy Word, and seek earnestly and urgently the mind of the Spirit, not only in this matter of baptism, but relating to all the doctrines of God's grace, that God's people may close their ranks, and together turn "to flight the armies of the aliens" (Heb.11: 34) and send up an urgent cry to the God of heaven, and never hold our "peace day nor night" and "keep not silence, and give Him no rest, till He establish, and till He make Jerusalem (the Church) a praise in the earth" (Is.62: 6,7).

APPENDIX

Statements appear on pages 73 and 85 with which some people may not be entirely in agreement, though being in agreement generally with the paedobaptist understanding of the Scriptural doctrine of Christian baptism. On account of this, I propose to examine these statements in the light of arguments which have been propounded in support of a contrary opinion and interpretation. The two statements are as follows;— (Page 73) — "Mankind is individually responsible and answerable to God." ... "There is no Scriptural warrant for a person to exercise faith *on behalf of another*, however young that other may be. Every infant is under an inescapable duty to make an intelligent response to the Gospel, as soon as God gives him (or her) the ability to do so." (Page 85) — "the grounds for infant baptism are uniquely established on the certainty of the divine command , and not on the uncertainty of individual regeneration."

Before entering upon this discussion, and in order to clear the ground before us, and to make it evident that such a difference of opinion does in fact exist, I will quote from something that has been stated by a contender for this alternative interpretation, as follows:— "Those who believe that children brought up in truly Christian homes and fellowships must needs go through a later experience of regeneration seem to us to miss the radical significance of Biblical and evangelical infant baptism." The root of this assertion is the belief that a person can exercise faith on behalf of an infant, which the statement on page 73 denies.

I am not at all certain that we should be discussing the subject of regeneration at this particular point at all. The spiritual state of an infant is something that has been deliberated upon by godly men, who have tried to resolve the mystery by introducing the notion of "the germ of faith", and by describing the situation as being one where "intelligent faith cannot be in exercise", and all this in order to explain how an infant may be regenerate. But as the spiritual state of an individual (particularly an infant) is something that frail mortals can never determine with certainty, it would seem to be more reasonable, rather, to follow tracks which are clearly discernible in the Scriptures.

Perhaps we should ask ourselves what our concern is. Why do we turn to speculation rather than revelation? Do we feel that if we cannot claim an infant to be regenerate it never will be later? God has appointed means to this end, but to exercise faith *on behalf of* an infant is not one of those means. The parents' faith is to be very much in exercise, but it is to be employed in *other* ways, in compliance with the terms of the Covenant — applying the external sign, praying, teaching and testifying by example.

The Scripture relating to the beneficial influence that a believing wife (or husband) *may* have upon her (or his) unbelieving partner (I Cor. 7:16) could very aptly be applied to the beneficial influence that believing parents *may* have upon their infant seed — "What knowest thou, O parent, whether thou shalt save thy child?" Which expression is one of *hope*, and not of *certainty*.

We know from the Scriptures that God *will* accomplish "the good pleasure of His will" (Eph. 1:5), by which "will" He determines the eternal destiny of each one of us , from infancy onwards, and even before infancy. Paul, who was not regenerate when an infant, said of himself, in retrospect, under the Spirit's inspiration — "When it pleased God, who separated me from my mother's womb, and called me by His grace" (Gal. 1:15). God separated him, even before he was born. This was something that was done in *eternity*. Then he was born, and grew up, and later, looking back on his earlier life, reckoned himself to be "Chief" of sinners — yet God had separated him from his mother's womb. God knew what He was doing, for later on He "called" him. That was something that was done in *time*, and stands out in the testimony of Scripture as an example of what God can do with a sinner "when the fulness of the time is come". The same is true of Jeremiah (Jer. 1:5). And we could mention also Isaiah (49:1).

Indeed we can say the same thing about all God's true people – separated in eternity by God's changeless decree, for their names "were written in the book of life from the foundation of the world" (Rev. 17:8).

There are certainly obligations and privileges which God has placed upon Christian families under the terms of the Covenant of Grace. This is the area where we must concentrate our thoughts and endeavours, and exercise our faith by the enabling grace of God; and moreover, we do not need to speculate upon the secret processes of the human heart, be it of an adult *or* an infant, for these are utterly beyond our power to determine.

Now let us look at the Scriptural grounds that it is claimed support the alternative interpretation, and provide proof that a person *can* exercise faith on behalf of another person, regardless of age, such as will result in the immediate conversion of that other person.

One such Scripture is Matthew 9:2 "Jesus seeing their faith said unto the sick of the palsy; Son, be of good cheer; thy sins be forgiven thee". It is said that the word "their" refers only to the four people bearing the "man sick of the palsy, lying on a bed". But why should it be limited to the four? It would seem to be much more natural for it to refer to the five. They were *all* adults. There is no reason why we should conclude that the one on the bed was incapable of thinking. No doubt all five had agreed together to go to Jesus who saw their faith. "He knew what was in man". Jesus would never commit Himself to anyone who had no faith. See John 2:23–25. In this case which we are considering He knew that the cripple's four helpers were men of faith, and He knew that the "one sick of the palsy" had faith to believe in Him, otherwise He would not have said "Son, thy sins be forgiven thee". The cripple knew that Jesus was able to forgive *him*, a guilty sinner. The commentaries corroborate this interpretation.

Another Scripture that has been used as warrant for this alternative interpretation is Joshua 24:15 "choose you this day whom ye will serve; ..... as for me and my house, we will serve the LORD". Those who cite this Scripture in support of the alternative interpretation, put the emphasis upon "me and my house", and I agree that "house" stands for household, including the children. It is suggested that Joshua gave his household no option. *He* decided *for* them. His faith embraced them all. As we consider this passage in its historical context we see that it describes a general assembly of the heads of the congregation of Israel, shortly before Joshua's death. He was opening the way for the people willingly to serve the LORD as a deliberate personal choice, and to reject the heathen gods, and he was setting them an example. "And the people said unto Joshua, The LORD our God will we serve, and His voice will we obey" (verse 24). The nation of Israel in those days was, in a unique way, a theocracy. Jehovah was their King, who looked for loyalty from all His subjects. This piece of Israelitish history can scarcely provide solid ground on which to base such a radical principle, related to New Testament church practices, as the one we are considering.

Another Scripture which has been used to support this alternative interpretation is Acts 16:31 "Believe on the Lord Jesus Christ, and thou shalt be saved, and thy house". The argument used is, that by the faith of this *one* man, the Philippian jailor, God saved *the whole family*. But that is not the case. The individual members of his family were to *be* saved, by faith in the same Saviour as was the jailor himself. We are told that Paul and Silas "spake unto him the word of the Lord, and to all that were in his house". Teaching had to be given before conversion.

Those I believe are the passages of Scripture which are mainly referred to in order to prove the validity of the opinion that faith may effectually be exercised by a parent on behalf of an infant, which will result in the conversion of the infant, and I believe that I have shown that support for such a view is not forthcoming from these Scriptures.

But it is evident , on account of the great weight that is placed upon the role played by *faith* in this matter, that we are obliged to examine, very closely, the *nature* of this faith. What sort of faith is it that is exercised by believing parents, on behalf of their infants, and which is claimed to be instrumental in saving those infants? It must surely be *justifying* faith. So let us consider the nature of justifying faith.

Justifying faith is a taking or receiving, what is held out to us in the Gospel, concerning the person and work of the Lord Jesus Christ, for the recovery and salvation of lost sinners. In justifying faith there is an assent to all divine and supernatural revelation, upon the testimony of God, the Revealer. It is not merely an assent of the mind, but also of the heart. In other words, justifying faith is that act of the soul whereby a convinced sinner looks to Christ, as He has been made a propitiation for his sins. He, and all that He is, and all that He has done, for the salvation of sinners, is the proper *object* of justifying faith. And how does a person come to know about that? It is by the Scriptures, the Word of God. A person believes the Scriptures to *be* the Word of God with a faith that is divine and supernatural. And how is a person brought into a condition in which he may benefit from the provisions that are made for sinners in Christ? He is made to see his *need* of Him. There must first be a work of *conviction of sin,* a sense of great and urgent need, the creation of a desire, a longing, for forgiveness and for life.

Having looked, in general terms, at the *nature* of justifying faith — the faith that must be exercised in order that a person may be justified — let us superimpose this understanding on the case of an infant who has received the sign and seal of the Covenant. We must ask ourselves what sort of faith it is that a parent exercises, which results in the salvation of his (or her) infant. What is the *object* of *that* faith? Is it the Saviour of sinners? But such a person, a parent, cannot look on Him as *his* Saviour for this particular purpose, but as someone else's Saviour — the infant's. But in *that* case where does conviction of sin come in? The infant, all will agree, is a sinner, a guilty sinner ("I was shapen in iniquity; and in sin did my mother conceive me" — Ps. 51:5). What do we do with the infants's sin? The infant cannot be convicted of sin, that would be unnatural. The dominion of sin in the heart is the most terrible and damning problem of the human race. God has revealed His way of dealing with it, by "Jesus Christ, and Him crucified", and there is no other way which He has revealed to us. Therefore there is no other ground for justifying faith to rest upon, and that must be preceded by conviction of sin, and by trusting, cleaving, personal, faith in Him. We can go no further than that. We are called upon to obey God's commands and fulfil our duties, as revealed in His Word, and we must leave the final issues to Him.

I will now give some consideration to the interpretation itself, which considers that the Scriptures justify the exercise of faith on the part of a parent as the means of bringing about the salvation of his (or her) infant, and I propose to do this in the light of the rite of circumcision, which, as we are agreed, is the Old Testament counterpart of the New Testament rite of baptism. There is an *exact* parallel between them. The purpose they served was the same in both cases. I have considered this subject fairly fully in the book and therefore aim to be brief here.

We see baptism mirrored in circumcision. Abraham was commanded by God to circumcise Ishmael. Ishmael therefore enjoyed the *privileges* of the Covenant. But Ishmael, in later years, proved not to be a man of faith. Those who say that a person's salvation depends on the faith of another, will say that Abraham cannot have exercised faith in the case of Ishmael. The sort of explanation that is given to rationalise such a situation in this Christian era is along these lines — "presumably the infant's parents were unable to believe for his salvation in this case." But I feel that this is not an adequate explanation. It is too vague, too tenuous, too groundless. It is based on something that goes on in a man's heart. In this connection, notice how Abraham felt about Ishmael — "O that Ishmael might live before Thee". Also notice what God said in response — "As for Ishmael, I have heard thee: Behold, I have blessed him". (Gen. 17:18, 20). I think that most would agree that in the light of those Scriptures Abraham must have *longed* for the salvation of Ishmael, and his faith must have been in keeping with that longing. Why did his faith fail at this point then (if it did do)? Was it a weakness on Abraham's part? But his faith must have been effective in the case of Isaac.

We must here make a dogmatic, and Scripturally warranted statement. God has *never* placed the eternal destiny of *any* individual in the hands of a frail, fallible, sinful man. *Never*. Man does not even co-operate in the work, in any *vital* way, otherwise he would prove to be the weak link that caused the chain to break. It may be said that it was God who ordered the faith of Abraham to be effective in the case of Isaac and not in the case of Ishmael. We can be sure of the fact that the matter was determined by God, and *that* being so, why do we bring Abraham and his faith into this area of mystery at all, which is God's own sovereign demesne?

Abraham was clearly circumscribed by certain well defined directions. He was under God's orders to do two specific things — (1) "Every man child among you shall be circumcised" (Gen.

17:10). (2) He must "command his children and his household after him, and they shall keep the way of the LORD, to do justice and judgment" (Gen. 18:19). The word "command" here has the sense of "instruct." No order was given to him about exercising faith on behalf of his children.

God included Abraham's unbelieving offspring with him within the Covenant, and as we have just observed, He required certain specific duties to be carried out by Abraham with respect *to* his offspring. And the same is true of the Christian family. The unbelieving infant is included within the Covenant for the sake of the parents. And this puts the infant into the same realm of *privilege* as the children of Abraham were in. For the sake of clarity of thought and action we must recognise the fact that Christian parents in this New Testament era are subject to the same commands that God gave to Abraham. Two things are required to be done, which are quite clear, crisp and specific. There is no uncertainty and no ambiguity here. They must (1) Ensure that their infants receive the sign of the Covenant — baptism. (2) Pray for and instruct their baptised infant in the ways of God and His "so great salvation."

Now as we consider the case that has just been described, it appears, on the face of it, to be the same as that which appertains in the case of those who believe that an infant can be saved by the faith of its parents. I say the two cases *appear* to be the same, because in both cases there is an obligation on the part of the parents to ensure that the infant receives the sign and seal of the Covenant, and there is equally an obligation on the part of the parents to pray for, and give instructions to, the infant. Where is the difference then? The difference is discovered in the fact that the two cases rest upon different criteria. The substance of the parents' prayers for their infants differs. In one case it is assumed that the great goal of regeneration has already been reached. So what can be the substance of prayers in that case? Well it seems that it is a matter of telling God that their infants are His and asking Him to keep them. You are exhorted under these circumstances to keep God to His Covenant, and to pray to that end.

But in the case of those who see their infants in the Covenant, and who do not presume anything concerning their infants' spiritual state, but who recognise that they are in a very privileged position, *they* have solid ground and great encouragement to pray for their children's *salvation*, because they are in a favoured position in the sight of God. Their children's *salvation* is the great burden of their prayers for them. But they are not *presumed* to be regenerate. This whole situation is based on sound and specific and well defined Biblical principles. The situation is such that the parents are under a continual obligation to pray for the salvation and sanctification of their infant seed, and to live out their lives in their sight "as it becometh the Gospel of Christ" (Phil. 1:27). Each parent aiming, by the grace of God, to be "an example of the believers, in word, in conversation, in charity, in spirit, in faith, in purity" (1 Tim. 4:12). Furthermore, they are also required to give them instructions in the Scriptures, so that they may come to realise that it is from *that* source that the message of hope comes. In other words, they are to bring up their children "in the nurture and admonition of the Lord" (Eph. 6:4). The ultimate issue is, as always, in God's hands.

Those who trust in their own faith for their children's salvation, will find themselves resting on unstable ground. They will find their faith to be a "broken reed" (Isaiah 36:6). However, in spite of this, on many occasions, by the grace of God, such infants grow up into Christian adults. But there *are* exceptions. And this is where the uncertainty lies. Why is there a *single* exception? The principle tells us that our children are regenerate on account of our faith. If they grow up and it then becomes evident that they are *not* regenerate, we ask ourselves what has gone wrong? It must be our faith. But we thought our prayers were as fervent as they could possibly be. How then can I *ever* be certain.

Would it not be wiser, and more Scriptural, to face up to the fact that as far as you are able to judge, although your infant is included in the Covenant, and given the sign and seal of the Covenant, it is not necessarily regenerate, and must not be presumed to be so? It *may* be one of God's elect people, we do not know, this is one of "the secret things that belong unto the LORD our God" (Deut. 29:29). We do not know *that*, but what we *do* know, beyond a shadow of doubt, is that the infant, being in the Covenant, is in a very privileged position. A place of prominence in God's sight.

★ ★ ★

An observation has also been made concerning the statement, appearing on page 50, that the Covenant of Grace relates to those people whose names are written in the Lamb's book of life, and to them alone. The observation made, suggests that this statement confuses the Covenant of Grace (made with believers and their children, but not necessarily with the elect) with the Covenant of Redemption (made between the Father and the Son).

This issue touches on a most vital point in connection with the Covenant of Grace, concerning which much confusion has arisen. When considered in an absolute sense, and bearing in mind its eternal and spiritual nature, the Covenant of Grace is that undertaking that God has entered into with all *believers*, in Christ, who is their federal Head.

Bearing *that* in mind, it is also important to take into account the fact, which I have emphasised in this book generally, that the professing Christian Church, by its very constitution, is made up of people who have made an intelligent and consistent profession of faith in Christ (see page 33). But in certain cases some of those people may prove not to be vitally united to ''the true vine'' (John 15:1 etc) (see page 31). There is therefore an administrative application of the Covenant of Grace to those who enjoy the *privileges* which it affords, in the realm of the professing Church, which privileges relate only to *time*, and not to *eternity*. If those privileges, are not taken advantage of (or ''improved'', as the Puritans would say) in *time*, they will have no value in *eternity*.

This then is the reasoning lying behind the statement made on page 50. The Covenant of Grace, in its ultimate purpose and accomplishment, is made with those people who enjoy Covenant privileges in *time*, and who *also* go on to enjoy the spiritual blessings of the Covenant in *eternity*. And those people are the elect of God.

This dual application of the Covenant is perfectly illustrated in the case of Ishmael, who bore the sign and seal of the Covenant, but did not go on to enjoy the everlasting blessings of glory which God promises to His elect people, under the terms of the Covenant of Grace.

INDEX OF SCRIPTURE REFERENCES

1 CORINTHIANS

2 CORINTHIANS

GALATIANS

EPHESIANS

PHILIPPIANS

COLOSSIANS

2 THESSALONIANS

1 TIMOTHY

2 TIMOTHY

GENERAL INDEX